Education, "Artificial" Intelligence, and Cognition

Kaustuv Roy

Education, “Artificial” Intelligence, and Cognition

Pedagogic Imperatives and the Coming Community

palgrave
macmillan

Kaustuv Roy
TIET Campus
Thapar Institute of Engineering and Technology
Patiala, Punjab, India

ISBN 978-3-031-82262-9 ISBN 978-3-031-82263-6 (eBook)
https://doi.org/10.1007/978-3-031-82263-6

This Palgrave Macmillan imprint is published by the registered company Springer Nature Switzerland AG.
The registered company address is: Gewerbestrasse 11, 6330 Cham, Switzerland

Acknowledgments

This book is greatly indebted to the pathbreaking work of the Spanish philosopher Xavier Zubiri (1898–1983), a prominent member of the Madrid School. There are numerous other voices and shoulders of the Great on whom the book rests, such as the work of the scientist Werner Heisenberg. I can only humbly thank these colossal spirits for their endless potentialities and their creative becomings that provide inspiration and sustenance to people like ourselves.

Contents

CHAPTER 1

Introduction: In-Quest of Intelligence

It would perhaps be quite an understatement to say that formal thinking about intelligence is fraught with difficulties, for the activity amounts to thought reflecting on itself, engaging in navel-gazing that makes the exercise circular and epistemically doubtful. This might be taken to be a kind of internal perspective—a view from within the phenomenon. From an external and social perspective, we are often reminded of the contentious nature of this referent by the considerable hackle-raising and hoof-digging by those who regard the construct with a certain suspicion. For what indeed could offer greater room for misgiving than the circularity involved in *mentally* ascribed labels about the *mental*.

> Even in the field of AI, definitions of intelligence are often consciously avoided, though there has been no shortage of attempts at formulations that make sense when speaking of artificial intelligence. Max Tegmark, for instance, defines intelligence as the ability to accomplish complex goals, and general intelligence as the ability to accomplish virtually any goal, including learning. But what does it mean to have a goal? These appear to be philosophical questions, and scientific communities are often impatient with such concerns. In Pei Wang's article *What do you mean by AI?* (2008), she investigated the matter, and concluded that there existed two widespread opinions on the concept of intelligence. One view was that there exists a natural definition of intelligence, and that different understandings in various schools of artificial intelligence merely deal with different aspects, while they approach the same subject. The other common attitude was to view

K. Roy, *Education, "Artificial" Intelligence, and Cognition*, https://doi.org/10.1007/978-3-031-82263-6_1

intelligence as a concept that *escapes definition*, and that it does not matter what researchers think about this.[1]

The circularity is perfectly captured above. Intelligence is the ability to accomplish complex goals, but the complexity of a goal, and even the very goal itself, involves a certain order of mental judgment that is generally considered to be in the realm of intelligence. In fact, the difficulty is so great that in another view, the term is best left undefined. In other words, when it comes to intelligence, we literally do not know what we are talking about. And to confound the issue further: "The word intelligence seems to take on different meanings in different contexts, and confusion is inevitable when those different meanings are implied within the same context. Will we have true artificial intelligence in 20 years? Well, the answer to that depends on … what we mean when we say intelligent."[2] All of this would not matter so much but for the fact that intelligence is an officially recognized and quantified term and evaluative assessments are routinely hung on its peg. Therefore, and against the portentousness of unrequited impressions, I feel pressed upon to take recourse to opening our discussion with a preliminary list of queries, by way of an attempt to get a foothold on the slippery slope of this abstruse notion together with its pervasiveness. Alongside, I hasten to seek the reader's indulgence in order to extend an invitation to accompany me into the undergrowth of questions thus provoked.

To begin with, for example, we can ask: Is intelligence symbolic or energetic? Is it ontological or is it epistemic? Is it a projection or is it an introjection? Is it a description, or is it an attribution? Is it intrinsic or is it extrinsic, is it subjective or objective? Is it unconditional or situational? Is it developmental or static? Is it individual or collective? Is it formulated in order to silence ab initio, or is it possible to speak of it in a critical spirit? Is it of the nature of a transcendental signified, and do we all mean the same thing by it? Further, how is its existence singularly determined? If not, then is it a reflexive construct of the elite—cooked up to maintain privilege, a safe barrier for ensuring social reproduction, an enclosure to keep others out? Who is likely to back the so-called Intelligence Quotient or IQ? Is it, as Gramsci might have put it, just another idea of the ruling

[1] Even Oygarden, *What is Intelligence? A Proposed Framework of four Different concepts of Intelligence* (Grimstad, Norway: University of Agder, 2019), p. 9.

[2] Ibid.

classes used for perpetuating soft domination? Or, is intelligence to be seen biologically in terms of evolutionary advantage over other species or even intra-species? What are its structural nature and its functional achievement? Has its operation been beneficial for the species and planetary life as a whole, or has it merely succeeded in controlling diversity? What is its connection to what we call instinct or intuition? Does the attribution of intelligence alter social relationalities through special credit? Is intelligence related to well-being or just being clever? Might intelligence be employed for destructive and nefarious purposes, or are there in-built restraints and warnings? Is there a useful measure of intelligence, or are there as many as you like? How do we make sense of the so-called multiple intelligences? And lastly, what is one to make of the prosthetic kind that today goes by the tag of "artificial intelligence"? What are the social and educational consequences of legitimating this nomenclature through usage?

One thing is clear from all of the above that, at the very least, the construct has the potential to raise a lot of doubts and concerns. Hence, it is imperative that a careful deconstruction of the same is carried out before we can get down to the specificities that concern the present inquiry. In other words, we need to first clarify what we mean by intelligence at the level of normal discourse before we can go on to address the increasing buzz around artificial intelligence. And second, the book needs to establish if this construct has anything really to do with education, and if so, what is the nature and quality of this relation. For, to begin with, we do not ask if the heart is intelligent, or the lungs, the kidneys, or the liver, for that matter, even as they carry out the most intricate tasks with alacrity and self-correction. They seem to be doing their jobs fairly well in most cases, irrespective of race, class, gender, culture, time, or space. In other words, competent biological functioning is generally taken for granted most of the time irrespective of social and cultural differences. Why then is it necessary or pertinent to posit what seems like a gratuitous construct by the name of intelligence in respect of mental functioning? Why can't the mind-brain be supposed to do its job like its other organic counterparts, without having to have brownie points attributed to it? But before we can proceed to inquire into these and other intriguing questions, it might be useful to take a quick peek into what thoughtful folks have had to say about this thing called intelligence. Below are a few selections presented for our consideration.

> [Intelligence is] the ability to carry out abstract thinking (Terman, 1921); the capacity for knowledge, and knowledge possessed (Henmon, 1921); the capacity to learn or to profit by experience (Dearborn, 1921); the capacity to acquire capacity (Woodrow, 1921); the power of good responses from the point of view of truth or facts (Thorndike, 1921); sensory capacity, capacity for perceptual recognition, quickness, range or flexibility of association facility and imagination, span of attention, quickness or alertness in response (Freeman, 1921); ability to learn or, having learned, to adjust oneself to the environment (Calvin, 1921); ability to adapt oneself adequately to relatively new situations in life (Pentler, 1921); a biological mechanism by which the effects of a complexity of stimuli are brought together and given a somewhat unified effect in behavior (Peterson 1921); the capacity to inhibit an instinctive adjustment, the capacity to redefine the inhibited instinctive (Thurstone, 1921); adjustment in light of imaginally experienced trial and error, and the capacity to realize the modified instinctive adjustment in overt behavior to the advantage of the individual as a social animal; Sensation, perception, association, memory, imagination, discrimination, judgment, and reasoning (Haggerty, 1921); the general ability or form of mental power that develops in the first five years of life to remain relatively stable after that (Boring, 1923); a global concept that involves an individual's ability to act purposefully, think rationally, and deal effectively with the environment (Wechsler, 1953); the ability to use optimally limited resources—including time—to achieve goals. (Kurzweil, 1999)[3]

We can see that the notions employed are largely positivistic, often assuming the very thing that needs to be explained, and entirely without a critical moment. Beyond these, I offer another account which is at a variance from the above in that it acknowledges that the so-called intelligence is a "construct," and while there appears to be something differentiable and measurable, nothing much can be said about it without examining the "latent processes" that underlie the construct and the attendant difference in observable behavior.

> Although intelligence is only an inferred notion, that is, a latent construct, it does refer to observable behavior. The extent to which intelligence is or is not a meaningful concept will therefore depend on empirical data or observable behavior. Typically, this behavior is measured in terms of individual differences in standardized performance on tests correlated with real-life

[3] Tomas Chamorro-Premuzzic & Sophie von Stumm (Eds.), *Wiley-Blackwell Handbook of Individual Differences* (London: Blackwell Publishing, 2015), p. 65.

outcomes, such as academic exam grades or job performance. Thus, the key issue is not whether we measure "intelligence" but whether we have found something worth measuring (Miles, 1957). As shown in Figure 5.2, the notion of intelligence is directly inferred from the relationship between test scores (e.g., IQ points) and other criteria, such as performance in school or at work. If these are significantly correlated, we can assume that intelligence has similarly affected both test performance and school/job performance. Any definition of intelligence will also have to conceptualize the underlying or latent processes that cause individual differences in test and school/job performance. Definitions of intelligence will be examined more closely throughout this chapter, but for an overview and preliminary understanding of the concept it should suffice to define it as a "general ability to reason, plan, solve problems, think abstractly, learn quickly, and learn from experience" (Gottfredson, 2000, p. 81). Intelligence, then, does not refer to specific abilities but to an "indivisible quality of mind that influences the execution of all consciously directed activities" (Robinson, 1999, p. 720).[4]

Delinking intelligence from specific capacities, the authors importantly liken it to an "indivisible quality of mind." Now, this leads to a significant contradiction, for, to my understanding, measurement is predicated upon defining of limits, that is upon isolation and separation—one cannot hope to measure that which is indivisible. We can measure heart rate or blood pressure, but we cannot measure health for the same reason. In other words, holistic notions are not measurable, precisely because there is no measure of holism; measurement is predicated upon atomism. Indivisible qualities are qualitative and not quantifiable, and hence preclude measurement by definition. Any attempt to quantify quality is bound to end up in contradiction of one kind or another. And therefore, we find that the epistemological minefield is often side-stepped by setting up the focus on testing.

A history of intelligence is largely a history of intelligence testing, that is, an account of psychology's attempt to quantify and measure individual differences underlying performance in an objective, scientific manner. In the words of René Descartes (1596–1650), a French philosopher and one of the most influential figures of modernity, "If something exists, it exists in some amount. If it exists in some amount, then it is capable of being measured." Accordingly, differential psychologists have dedicated themselves, in particular during the first half of the twentieth century, to designing psychometric

[4] Ibid., p. 66.

> instruments to com pare individuals on what they believed were the most important aspects of human intellect: intelligence.[5]

Why could we not entertain or name other aspects of the human intellect or psyche as intelligence? Again, why do we not, for instance, consider an attitude of compassion or a keen sense of justice as intelligent behavior? At this point, it is too early to even attempt to address these choices for these are complex issues that need to be opened up gradually. And so let us turn back to the questions we stated at the beginning.

The first question on our list is an ontological one: Is intelligence symbolic or energetic? In other words, does it consist primarily of representative and logical-connective capacity whose context is provided by the existing universe of social meanings, or is it a movement of energy leading to changes in the intensity of the being? In other words, is intelligence a measure of the representational correspondences in a mental sphere, that is, constitutive of a certain mapping of reality, or has it something to do with the psycho-somatic magnification of the organism? Let us look into this question by stepping back a little in history.

> In 1904, the French Ministry of Public Instruction commissioned Alfred Binet to develop a method of identifying children with learning difficulties. Rather than relying on teachers' assessments, which were often biased against children with discipline problems, the French government wanted a method that effectively discerned capable pupils from less capable pupils. This implicit distinction between behavioral problems (such as absenteeism and disruptive behavior) and learning difficulties (such as lack of understanding of subjects) illustrates the differences between the realms of personality and intelligence. Binet (Binet & Simon 1905/1961a) believed that whilst personality describes and predicts individuals' behavior in and outside the classroom, intelligence would explain school performance based on the requirements to learn, understand, and relate concepts, theories, and methods acquired in the classroom.[6]

This was an early attempt to systematically isolate the mental from the behavioral in the educational domain and identify intelligence with the former through and by means of assessing school performance. The differential grasp of the official curriculum came to be an indicator of "diverse

[5] Ibid., p. 68.
[6] Ibid., p. 67.

levels of intelligence," eventually coming to be seen as a stable measure of this isolated factor. We can see the circular logic in operation: thought names a characteristic with regard to its own functioning, and then assigns a scale of values with regard to that functioning, which, in turn, settles the reality of the phenomenon. The positivistic pragmatism begins to form an overlay obscuring the uncertain conceptual progression, as it marches toward a comprehensive self-validation.

> Binet's advances in psychological testing were undoubtedly a consequence of his pragmatic approach to individual differences in intelligence and school achievement. To Binet, intelligence was all about practical sense and adaptation to the real world. Instead of starting from a theoretical or experimental perspective accounting for intrapsychic processes and sensorial operations, like Galton and J. M. Cattell, Binet adopted a commonsense applied approach whose goal was specifically the design of an effective, robust tool to predict differences in school performance. Rather than observing people's reactions to meaningless stimuli, Binet gave his subjects real tasks such as reading the time or completing a sentence. More importantly, Binet's predictive tool allowed educators to compare learning potential at a very early age (i.e., 4 years), irrespective of previous instruction. Binet was nonetheless very cautious about the usefulness of his measure and the meaning of what it assessed, as illustrated in his comprehensive definition of intelligence which has stood the test of time: "It seems to us that in intelligence there is a fundamental faculty, the alteration or the lack of which, is of the utmost importance for practical life. This faculty is judgment, otherwise called good-sense, practical sense, initiative, the faculty of adapting one's self to circumstances. A person may be a moron or an imbecile if he is lacking in judgment; but with good judgment he can never be either. Indeed, the rest of the intellectual faculties seem of little importance in comparison with judgment." (Binet & Simon, 1916/1973, pp. 42–43)[7]

What seems to surface from the above statement of Binet with regard to the special mental faculty is the capacity for judgment. Now, the question that immediately arises is what is "judgment" and how is it to be assessed? According to the Merriam-Webster Thesaurus, there are at least forty-two synonyms and cognate words for judgment in the English language. Even without quibbling about meaning, we can see that judgment is highly subjective, especially in non-trivial situations. For instance, an action that is deemed foolhardy with the advantage of hindsight, might

[7] Ibid., p. 69.

have been labeled as a case of remarkable judgment had it come off. Besides, judgmental capacity assessed with the help of two-dimensional, pen-and-paper tasks, need not be transferable into the four-dimensionality of life situations and relations. We have innumerable instances of seemingly well-educated people doing absurd and inexplicable things when it involves higher judgment in real-life situations. In other words, judgment is highly contextual and variable, even for the same person temporally, spatially, as well as relationally. And to hope for a scale that might formally and reliably assess judgment between persons is no different than the original task of determining intelligence.

> Aware of the limitations of his scale, Binet called for qualitative research on the developmental aspects of intelligence, a call later addressed by one of his students, Jean Piaget. In addition, Binet thought his scale could only provide a sample of all intelligent behaviors, and that its use was limited to a few samples that shared a certain cultural background. Indeed, a shared cultural background was certainly necessary to provide individuals with the knowledge to solve most of Binet–Simon's tests. As it was, then, such doubts discouraged Binet from claiming to have found a measure of any fundamental capacity: "I have not sought in the above lines to sketch a method of measuring, in the physical sense of the word, but only a method of classification of individuals. The procedures which I have indicated will, if perfected, come to classify a person before or after such another person, or such another series of persons; but I do not believe that one may measure one of the intellectual aptitudes in the sense that one measures a length or a capacity." (Binet, quoted in Varon, 1936, p. 41)[8]

Cognitive behavior in the young and the behavior of the mature individual are worlds apart if only due to the exponentially higher number of variables and their interrelationships involved in the latter. To play with glass beakers or colored liquids under controlled conditions is a qualitatively different exercise than behavior under actual constraints and live tensions. Jean Piaget's well-known experiments with children of a certain age and socio-cultural background may have elicited scientific interest and inspired some to probe further in the cognitive direction, but examined against the complexity of relations within dynamic settings the results could only be of formal academic interest. Specifically, they do not throw any light on what is intelligence within complex relational activity that is

[8] Ibid.

changing from moment to moment. Binet seems to have increasingly despaired of finding a concrete measure of intelligence, and so his modified approach began to fall back on creating a hierarchy instead. That is to say, his attempts now began to focus on placing people on a relative scale or ladder in which one might be higher or lower than another around certain chosen performatives. But, interestingly, even in doing so, he warned that it should not be seen as an objective measure of anything such as, for instance, breadth or depth, but only as difference. In contemplating intelligence historically therefore, we right away find ourselves on dubious and slippery grounds, for no less a reason than that the very creators of the concept admit to its deficiencies and doubtful meaning. Not supported by anything ontological (i.e., necessity), intelligence from the outset has remained an artifice, even an arbitrary mode of exclusion, that disprivileges alternative ways of being and thinking. Nevertheless, popular perception, socialized and molded by ruling discourses, believes in its reality, and besides, despite the fact that there is no consistent evidence that people deemed intelligent, in general, have been more valuable for planetary life, the positivity of intelligence has acquired lasting legitimacy. Further, there is now the eager narrative around an artificial variety that has gained immense social acceptance and discursive traction, whose mechanism and effect we have set out to scrutinize in these pages.

Let us go back to the questions we started with. I will pick as my first question: 'Is intelligence symbolic or energetic?' In other words, does intelligence comprise symbolic performance or does it involve the intensity of performance? To make the distinction clear, the former might include representational accuracy, logical connectivity, symbolic expansion, and informational acquirement. On the other hand, the latter alludes to existential vitality, intuitive sensuality, force of clarity, and depth of perception. But do these two clusters lie on opposite sides of a great divide? Not necessarily. Rather, it is the emphasis that determines the cluster upon which we are really focused. Modern discourse about intelligence mostly points toward the former, and we have already seen the historical reasons as to why that is the case. Also, the phenomenological dimension is deemphasized as it demands a freedom of interest that cannot easily be part of the routinization of life and formalization of learning which structurally leans toward manipulation of the symbolic order. As a result, measurement of intelligence exclusively reflects the efficiencies related to the symbolic order.

Why should this be regarded as an issue? When we measure "intelligence" in terms of levels of performativity within the symbolic order, we leave out the vast organo-affective context within which the performance is carried out. It is similar to the production of surplus value that Marx had noticed. Workers do not just carry out formally designated tasks, but perform against and within the backdrop of innate knowledges and phenomenological capabilities that are simply taken for granted and never compensated for. Similarly, an individual coming from a certain background of efficiencies and universe of meaning-making will interpret a task differently than a person with a different experiential background. In other words, background efficiencies and propensities acutely affect our performance in any domain and the performance by itself cannot be treated in isolation as something objective. Hence, in critically posing the question as to whether intelligence is primarily symbolic or affective, we come away decidedly undecided, even as formal descriptions of intelligence remains markedly associated with manipulations of the symbolic order. No doubt there has been protestations regarding emotional intelligence and so on, but at the end of the day, we are measured by our representational competence and not by the depth of our compassion.

The next question we will ask ourselves from our initial list is: Is intelligence a projection or introjection? But we have to first clarify what we mean by the terms of the question. What is projection and what is its connection to intelligence, and likewise for introjection? There is a concept in mathematics called regression. It refers to the degree of tendency for a group of values to "regress" or move toward the mean or average of those values. Abducting this notion in order to describe a seeming parallel in human tendencies, it is well-understood in social psychology that human individuals move toward adoption of generalized values and acceptances, or the social common denominator. It has been noted that in adolescence or even earlier, individuals hive off many of the divergences and creative differences from their personality in order to belong to the crowd, or to be seen as a "regular" guy or girl. This might include the best parts of our psychological selves such as kindness, generosity, and the sense of fairness. And equally, we suppress those parts of ourselves that are socially disparaged such as hatred, jealousy, and anger. In other words, in constructing our social selves and personality, we leave out those parts, positive or negative, that cannot be easily integrated, and that are not encouraged by primary and secondary agents of socialization that includes family and friends. This abjuring may be referred to as a process of alienation—we abandon those parts of ourselves that are socially suspect. Desperate to get approval and be accepted, we try to be liked by everyone whose opinion matters to us. Some writers have called this attempt to be normal, or average, or achieve the social mean, a “soul surgery.” Be that as it may, in actuality all of these hived-off parts of ourselves cannot really be got rid of, and instead become part of our repressed selves. They follow us around because they have nowhere to go—innate qualities that cannot be wished away merely by psychological reaction or suppression. So what is the mechanism by which we get around our repression? Our undesired characteristics in the repressed repository are sensed in others and projected onto them in a kind of unconscious casting, bouncing off the other and back to us as though independent and autonomous. To put it differently, we see in the other a reflection of our repressed parts, but in a way that appears as unconnected and independent. Both hero-worship and demonization feature in this gallery of projection. In general, we “experience” reality as independent of us, whereas it is, in large and significant ways, our own projection.

Introjection, on the other hand, is a process by which we internalize the other’s values and norms as our own even when these are quite contrary to our own values. This typically occurs under social duress and is a defense mechanism that serves to protect the self, such as when women identify with patriarchal values, or a victim identifies with the aggressor, and so on. We can no longer tell which part is our authentic self and which part is imported. This does not mean however that the two are easily reconciled. The inner conflict can lead to seriously maladaptive or self-destructive behavior. In terms of our concern here, a legitimized single-measure of mental hierarchy can result in conformism and the denial of authentic self. It can also lead to unpredictable and violent behavior that is the product of inner conflict.

In asking whether intelligence is a projection we are asking whether an immeasurable part of ourselves is repressed, projected, and eventually recuperated as a reflection from the external environment. On the other hand, in asking whether intelligence is an introjection, we are asking whether parts of our infinitely diverse and unique selves are socially and culturally overlaid with a standardized measure of something called intelligence, leading to subsidence of creative diversity. As with the question raised earlier, issues such as these are not easily answered or resolved, and while we can indicate, and be suggestive about, the direction of the problem, we will have to await their unfolding in the pages to come.

Next we will ask whether intelligence is intrinsic or extrinsic, that is to say, whether intelligence is biological or social. In other words, must we regard intelligence as an inner state or condition of the brain-mind or should we think of it as a culturally induced performative phenomenon. If we think of it as the former, that is, as intrinsic and biological, we run into the problem of making a transcendental claim of inherent hierarchies, a claim that cannot be empirically substantiated, as the structural differentiation of the brain is not well understood. At the same time, if we say that intelligence is cultural, that is to say, contextual, then that leads to the acknowledgment that a change of context would produce different results. But such an admission would take away the carefully constructed legitimacy that surrounds the notion. The history of intelligence tells us that apart from its military and espionage use, its invocation in the civic sphere has been directed at producing privileged or exclusionary lists. Hence any questioning of its legitimacy can destabilize the ruling order of things in the intellectual world.

The next big question that arises is: Is there any concrete reason to believe that the operation of intelligence has benefited planetary life in general which includes the human species but is not exhausted by it? In response to this difficult question it would be unwise to provide a summary assessment. That would be both hasty and premature at this stage of the inquiry. But one way to regard this question is to approach it anthropologically. From the self-description of societies who regard themselves as "advanced," we can try to analyze their planetary record as per certain criteria in which intelligence must be presumed or implicated. This can be compared to the planetary record of societies that are regarded as primitive or less advanced. Besides, against planetary life in general as the backdrop, we can begin by looking at the agenda of human intelligence that it has self-proclaimed and operationalized, especially those items that are both highly rewarded and socially regarded. But, before we can make any assessment we must also establish a positive link between so-called intelligence and social hierarchy. For establishing a theoretical link, we can take recourse to Marx's famous line that all ruling ideas are the ideas of the ruling classes. From that it follows that, since intelligence is a ruling idea, and it importantly determines the direction and deployment of resources of societies, it may be causatively linked to the consequences and performance of those ideas at the highest levels. And if these consequences are at odds with the health of planetary life in general then intelligence will have to face some sticky questions. To put it differently, has the record of intelligence in terms of conceptualizing, promoting, planning, and executing specific human agendas been anti- or pro-planetary-life? At this preliminary stage we cannot do much more than setting up the lines of our inquiry, while reiterating that intelligence cannot be separated from the *karma* of its promoters—we cannot lose sight of the consequences and record of their performance.

The question we will consider next is the following: Has intelligence any relation with instinct and intuition? To put it somewhat differently, is there a precursor to intelligence such as instinctive judgment and intuitive understanding or is intelligence an absolutely unprecedented phenomenon that makes its appearance at a certain point in evolutionary history? As with the earlier questions, this is also a difficult one to begin with, since intelligence could not possibly anticipate itself, nor can the mind look back easily upon its own history, or isolate the developmental emergence of any specific characteristic with regard to itself. However, we can survey the situation from the temporal perspective of the present, and see to what extent the problem remains the same, notwithstanding the passage of time. Consider the extract below, from an important study about the relation between insight and intelligence.

> An increasing body of evidence points to the important role of implicit processes and intuition in cognition, creativity, expertise, and decision making (Greenwald et al., 2002), (Dorfler & Ackermann, 2012; Pétervári, Osman, & Bhattacharya, 2016; Raidl & Lubart, 2001), (Klein, 2011). However, there is still little known about individual differences in intuitive abilities and their structure, and whether intuition is really 'the intelligence of the unconscious' (Gigerenzer, 2008; Kaufman, 2011). … Is there one intuition or are there more intuitive abilities? Can people differ in the extent to which they use and benefit from using their intuitions? In this study, we aimed to explore relationships between intuitive abilities, intelligence and personality. Moreover, is intuition a unitary psychological construct or, alternatively, a complex cognitive conglomerate that incorporates diverse processes and mechanisms. The majority of researchers agree that intuition predominantly operates implicitly, without cognitive control and awareness. Nevertheless, other characteristics of intuitive processes (for example, complexity, time, and metacognition) are disputable and depend on the phenomenon studied. We decided to define intuition as the ability to implicitly learn and detect

cognitive patterns, and to subconsciously combine information in complex ways to make correct judgments based on fragmentary cues.[9]

The above alludes to the binary or two-factor theory of perception, namely the implicit and the explicit, or a part which is largely unmodified and primal, and another which is more symbolic and representational. The former operates below the threshold of active awareness, whereas the latter functions subject to cognitive control. Both function simultaneously, to different extents based on circumstances (which are not fully understood), in order to bring about coherent and cogent perception-cognition.

> Intuition is based on various cognitive processes and mechanisms. One of the most fundamental and evolutionarily old of these is the ability to spontaneously acquire complex patterns on the basis of the procedural memory (i.e., implicit learning; Reber, 1993). For example, Reber (1967, 1993) showed that people can unintentionally learn artificial complex grammars (in the Artificial Grammar Learning task; AGL). Despite an absence of explicit knowledge about the rules, participants performed above the chance level (recognizing items as compatible vs. incompatible with a specific grammar), indicating the existence of implicit learning. Evidence for implicit learning has also been provided using different paradigms, for example, detecting hidden covariations (Lewicki, 1986; Lewicki, Hill, & Czyzewska, 1992) and by using the Serial Reaction Time task (SRT, Kaufman et al., 2010). Furthermore, intuitive abilities are likely to govern the integration of cues into a whole in a complex way, without aware access to this process. Individuals can correctly recognize things based on little information (Westcott, 1968a), or even subconsciously combine them in order to find new solutions.[10]

A gestalt-like grasp of situations and robust inferential capabilities within highly limited informational milieus is characteristic of intuitive processes. The most important attribute seems to be the capacity to integrate disparate fragments and come up with a complex whole (picture) that is meaningful and actionable.

[9] Agata Sobkow et al. "The structure of intuitive abilities and their relationships with intelligence and Openness to Experience," *Intelligence 67 (2018) 1–10*, https://doi.org/10.1016/j.intell.2017.12.001, downloaded April 17, 2024.

[10] Ibid.

> Even when people do not consciously know a solution, they can correctly guess which item is coherent with it (Bowers et al., 1990), and a solution to a problem can suddenly, and often surprisingly, appear in consciousness in the form of an insight. The latter effect is often accompanied by feelings of coherence, positive emotions and subjective certainty about the solution (Danek & Wiley, 2017; Nosal, 2011; Topolinski & Strack, 2009a, 2009b; Webb, Little, & Cropper, 2016). The ability to solve problems requiring insight is related to both convergent and divergent thinking, as well as to the ability to break a frame, allowing transitions between convergent and divergent thinking (DeYoung, Flanders, & Peterson, 2008). Furthermore, insightful individuals show greater diffuse activation in the visual cortex (which is related to more diffuse attention), and greater right hemisphere activation during resting-state EEG brain activity (Kounios et al., 2008; Kounios & Beeman, 2014), suggesting differences in brain structure.[11]

A word that is often used in association with intuition is insight. The latter is an intuitive leap that cannot be explained in terms of what is currently known about a problem phenomenon or its solution path. The sudden appearance in conscious thought of a solution that signifies a departure from the existing pattern of thought surrounding a problem, often leading to a more elegant solution, can be called insight. But is intuition or insight intelligence? And can it be anticipated or simulated? If the answer to that is negative, then the implication would be that intelligence of intuition can never be reproduced being solely an organic process whose secrets are destined to be outside the known—the moment something enters the known, it is dead and is no longer living intelligence. In other words, we can experience the effects of intuitive intelligence but can never get to its source or cause, which remains ostensibly outside our cognitive grasp. But of course, as yet we are nowhere near making any such categorical assertion, and have miles to go before anything definitive can be stated.

> The structure of intuition is still unexplored. Hogarth (2010) even believes that 'the greatest challenge facing intuition researchers is to determine more precise ways of classifying different types of intuitive phenomena' (p. 350). Historically, intuition was rather treated as an homogeneous construct. For example, Carl Jung defined it as a 'psychological function that unconsciously yet meaningfully transmits perceptions, explores the unknown, and senses possibilities which may not be readily apparent' (Hodgkinson et al., 2008,

[11] Ibid.

> p. 5; Jung, 2014), and placed it at the second end of a dimension of 'sensing': the direct receiving of information through the senses. On the other hand, dual-process theories view intuition as being opposed to a rational and analytical mode of processing (Evans, 2008; Kahneman, 2011; Stanovich & West, 2000). Importantly, most dual-process models have regarded intuition as a unitary construct, although, as an exception to this, Epstein and Pacini (Epstein & Pacini, 1999; Pacini & Epstein, 1999) in their Rational-Experiential Inventory (REI) distinguished two types of intuition: Experiential Ability and Experiential Engagement. However, such a distinction does not include the different types of processing that might plausibly underlie intuition, and only differentiates perceived ability from the motivation to use it.[12]

For the purposes of the present analysis, it is unimportant whether intuition is unitary or multiple. Rather, we are concerned with whether intuitive abilities and insight are core aspects of what we know as intelligence, and whether these can be analytically grasped and reproduced at will, or whether the processes are essentially outside our conscious comprehension, only available as effects.

> Much research on individual differences in cognitive abilities focuses on controlled and explicit tasks: working memory tests, verbal analogies, Raven's Matrices, etc. Nevertheless, the recent Dual-Process Theory of Human Intelligence (Kaufman, 2011) integrates dual-process theories of human cognition (Epstein, 2009; Evans, 2003; Kahneman, 2011) with the traditional approach to intelligence. It is argued that spontaneous and implicit cognition (related to intuition) is independent of, but complementary to, explicit cognitive ability or IQ (Danner, Hagemann, Schankin, Hager, & Funke, 2011; Kaufman, 2011; Nosal, 2011). Depending on task requirements, these two forms of cognitive abilities—explicit and implicit—dynamically interact, giving rise to intellectual functioning. Moreover, flexible switching between these two modes of cognition is likely to result in adaptive and optimal behavior. Indeed, empirical studies have revealed that implicit learning is largely independent of general intelligence showing no, or very low, relationships between AGL or SRT tasks performance and scores.[13]

[12] Ibid.
[13] Ibid.

The moment we recognize that intelligent functioning is the result of a dynamic interaction between two different forms of cognitive abilities—implicit and explicit—we are on our way to acknowledging that living intelligence may not be mimicked through backward engineering. In other words, we cannot work backward to the source from observing and mimicking the cognitive effects. To hope to do so is a bit like imagining that we can reconstruct the artist from the oeuvre; art is not merely an arrangement of technique and skill, but a mode of reception of inspiration. From this angle, even where AI is sold as a diminished cultural surrogate in many situations including pedagogic ones, we can see how uncreative is the construct when it comes to human flourishing.

The next question before us is whether intelligence is individual or collective. We are familiar with the terms of methodological individualism and the agentic perspective which individualizes capabilities. It would be more useful here to begin on the other side, that is, by examining the position surrounding the collectivist approach.

> We argue that it is more effective to understand intelligence as being collective "all the way down," so to speak. That is, for any apparent individual, closer inspection may reveal its intelligence to be instantiated by collective dynamics on a lower (and sometimes higher) scale of analysis. We propose several advantages of this approach: First, understanding intelligence as primarily a process enacted by groups places the study of intelligence on firmer ground for empirical research, basing the phenomenon in observable mechanisms, including networks of interactions, competition and cooperation dynamics, and consensus building. We argue that any mechanistic explanation of individual intelligence must ultimately fall back on such phenomena, and therefore it is unclear what is to be gained by separating individual and collective intelligence into distinct categories. Second, our perspective leaves an opening for a truly general theory of intelligence, without making prior assumptions about the type of system by which intelligence may be exhibited. Third, our perspective permits an evolutionary consideration of intelligence, focused on how the mechanisms of collective intelligence may be honed over generations to make groups smarter and more coherent. … We view intelligence as a process enacted by many interacting parts, rather than a property, and view the individual/collective distinction as a continuum, rather than a binary, determined by the relative interdependence of interacting parts.[14]

[14] J. Benjamin Falandays et al. "All intelligence is collective intelligence," *Journal of Multiscale Neuroscience, vol.2(1), 169–191*, DOI: https://doi.org/10.56280/1564736810.

Thinking of intelligence as lying in the interactive transfers within interdependent complexes is certainly a different way of viewing intelligence than seeing it as a property or characteristic or quality of an entity. What can this approach tell us? First it implies that intelligent is not a static concept but a dynamic process. Someone comes to me and seeks directions on teaching art to prisoners, capturing prison life in art. I have never thought of this before. Together we begin to think about it, but then realize that this would make much more sense if convicts themselves were asked to participate in the discussions. After plenty of negotiations we get to contact someone who is out on parole. Overcoming the initial hiccups and the lack of trust, we begin by asking whether this is at all a good idea. To put matters in a nutshell, initially we are met with contempt and derision and dismissed out of hand, but as we persist and argue beyond the conventional trappings and forms of art, there is a stirring of interest. There is a lot of energy, but there is also a lot of anger and frustration in a prison. But this is also true among artists. Can a little of this be mapped onto something? The answer to this question lay at the intersection of a multiplicity of minor awakenings that did not belong to anyone as a pre-given characteristic. What appeared eventually at the interactive node was that some could film aspects of prison life, a few would then select frames out of these, and subsequently, yet others suitably trained would engrave this in metal.[15] This emergence took months of negotiations between various parties, but what is most remarkable is that it was a co-emergence that took place one small move at a time. None of us could have guessed the outcome of these protracted negotiations. But what is evident is that all of us are in a better place than before as a result of what was jointly achieved. This is certainly not trivial. What was demonstrated by this joint exploration that began with plenty of hesitancy is the view of intelligence as a "process enacted by many interacting parts rather than a property," and a perspective that highlights "the individual/collective distinction as a continuum rather than a binary," determined by the interdependence of several units which themselves may be the intelligent result of other interacting parts. Arguably, this could lead to a more broad-based understanding and theorization of intelligence.

[15] Needless to say that these were not high security prisoners but inmates of a correctional home where they were permitted certain freedoms as well as the handling of tools.

> Our approach here is a form of argument-by-elimination: If it can be seen that mechanisms of intelligence at every level of analysis are best understood as collective behaviors, what is left to qualify as individual intelligence? Ultimately, we suggest that human brains occupy one end of a gradient in which a collective has become exceptionally interdependent, but that nonetheless operates according to mechanisms of collective intelligence that are present across species and scales of analysis. We hope that these considerations may help students of individual intelligence to recognize the value of seeing their phenomena of interest as emerging from collective dynamics, while simultaneously encouraging students of collective intelligence to recognize how collectives may come to act as individuals.[16]

It is possible that some interdependencies have become frozen into lasting semi-permanencies due to evolutionary imperatives, and as a consequence have begun to acquire a deceptively independent status. As an example, one can think of the organic brain as a collective in which the amalgamate has become exceptionally interdependent, "but that nonetheless operates according to mechanisms of collective intelligence that are present across species." Thus what is essentially a collective or a multiplicity may appear as an identity.[17] Why is it important to realize this multiplicity-in-identity? In order to release the potentialities innate in the interdependent parts, it becomes important to go beyond the bonded illusion so that the "binding energy" between the layers is freed up, as it were, and become fluidly available. What this means is that a partial dissolution of identity can bring about new ways of viewing objects and relations and therefore generate new alliances, amalgamates, and modes of intelligent behavior within fresh complexes.

[16] Benjamin Falandays et al., op. cit.

[17] Ibid. Further, Falandays et al. observe that: "The mind, and by extension intelligence, has traditionally been thought of as something possessed by individuals. However, eusocial insect colonies challenge the idea of intelligence as exclusively a property of an individual (Theiner, 2014). Colonies of ants, bees, and termites clearly display vastly greater and sometimes qualitatively distinct abilities compared to the individuals that they are composed of (Sumpter, 2006). Moreover, the intelligence of these collective units cannot simply be characterized as the sum of the intelligences of its constituents. The collective cognition and decision-making of the colony is determined by the interactions between the individuals, resembling mobile neural networks, and the algorithms that determine their output (Couzin, 2009). Thus, one approach to reconcile the intelligence of these colonies with individual intelligence may be by considering colonies as superorganisms (Wheeler, 1920) that parallel the intelligence and cohesive unity of a multicellular organism."

> The dynamics of collective intelligence in humans share deep commonalities with those of other systems. We emphasize that collective intelligence in humans actually has little to do with how intelligent we are as individuals, and instead to the extent to which we are evolutionarily prepared for spontaneous interpersonal coordination. As we saw in the last section that our brains—themselves intelligent collectives—adaptively resonate to patterns of stimuli in the environment, consider that sometimes that environment contains other humans. Thus, when multiple humans observe and interact with one another, they may become intertwined in a sensorimotor feedback loop, leading the group to exhibit complex, coordinative patterns, without requiring any individual to do anything all that intelligent in a traditional sense (e.g. planning, reasoning, storing information). Over the last two decades, a large body of literature has amassed demonstrating that individuals engaged in conversations or joint tasks tend to spontaneously align their linguistic behaviors and synchronize many rhythms of the body.[18]

Looking at it from the opposite end, an isolated proficiency will be dragged down by the surrounding mediocrity. We all know about the lowest common denominator in networks, which tend to adjust to the segment or node with the lowest efficiency within the interdependent group capability. This implies that units in interdependent groups are constrained by the level of co-efficiency embedded in the complex, and since almost all human social activity is in some way co-dependent, this makes the socially available functional intelligence implicitly that value which is attainable within the dynamics of the particular system. Hence it is meaningless to speak of an isolated intelligence.

> Decades of research in cultural evolution, anthropology, and other social and ecological sciences have posited that the "secret of our success" as a species is our capacity to learn collectively (Henrich, 2015; Laland, 2018). This

[18] Ibid. The authors further note that, "For example, it has been found that, over the course of some types of interactions, individuals entrain their neural oscillations (Montague et al., 2002; Konvalinka & Roepstorff, 2012), their postural sway (Shockley et al., 2003) and other movements (Richardson et al., 2007; Schmidt & O'Brien, 1997). Individuals also align their speech patterns at the level of pronunciation (phonetic convergence; Pardo, 2006), word choice (lexical alignment; Branigan et al. 2011), grammatical structure (syntactic alignment; Branigan et al., 2007), and speaking rate (Manson et al. 2013), as well as coordinate the position of their gaze (Richardson & Dale, 2005). Furthermore, human individuals may imitate each other's facial expressions (McIntosh, 2006), postures, gestures, etc. (Chartrand & Van Baaren, 2009). In some cases, patterns of synchrony emerge in groups even when individuals are not directly interacting."

> collective intelligence of human cultures has recently been called the "collective brain" (Muthukrishna & Henrich, 2016). The notion of the collective brain or collective intelligence has put into question many persistent myths about innovation and ingenuity. For instance, research has illustrated how innovation is to a large degree recombination, involving the reuse of pre-existing components in novel contexts (Muthukrishna & Henrich, 2016; Arthur, 2009). Science, too, is much less a feat of "lone geniuses" than a collective search process which involves high degrees of fiduciary relations and reapplication of previously useful solutions. … In such a context, truly "individual" learning must be exceedingly rare. Accordingly, some have argued that most learning is "hybrid learning": human individuals acquire skills through socially mediated trial and error and culturally evolved practice (Sterelny, 2012). Of course, one could argue that humans still have innate predispositions to be adept individual learners (see, e.g., Heyes, 2018), although research in gene-culture coevolution suggests that even our individual level cognitive mechanisms have likely been thoroughly shaped by our species' collective history as social animals.[19]

Looking into the history of science, for example, one can see how each discovery was dependent on some of the prior discoveries. The context of discovery is sometimes called a paradigm, and "though observation and questioning are essential to the process of science, they are not enough to launch a scientific investigation on their own. Generally, scientists also need scientific background knowledge—all the information and understanding they've gained from their scientific training in school, supplemented by discussions with colleagues and reviews of the scientific literature. An understanding of what other scientists have already figured out about a particular topic is critical to the process. This background knowledge allows scientists to cognize novel observations for what they are, to make connections between ideas and observations, and to figure out which questions can be fruitfully tackled with available tools. The importance of domain knowledge to the process of science helps explain why science is often mischaracterized as a systematic set of facts contained in textbooks. Science is a process, but one that relies on accumulated knowledge to move forward."[20] In this sense, no finding is entirely original—there are always ideational precursors to any discovery, be it Darwin's

[19] Ibid.

[20] UC Museum of Paleontology, *Understanding Science*, Downloaded @ https://undsci.berkeley.edu/understanding-science-101/how-science-works/exploration-and-discovery.

Theory of Evolution, or Einstein's Theory of Relativity, to mention but a couple. From the perspective of an inquiry into intelligence, it makes an important crack in the edifice of methodological individualism that sees, *inter alia*, big ideas as originating from individuals. It gives us an opening to inquire into processes that are richer and more complex than simply associating intelligence with individuals. An aside might be useful here: "The time is July 1885, the place Mount McGregor, to which the eighteenth president of the United States, Ulysses S. Grant, has retired to write his memoirs." On his deathbed, unable to speak because of the throat cancer that was killing him, Grant penciled the following note to his doctor, John H. Douglas. "The fact is I think I am a verb instead of a personal pronoun. A verb is anything that signifies to be; to do; or to suffer. I signify all three." There is no knowing what exactly was going through Grant's mind as he wrote these gnomic lines, for he died a few days later. My purpose in this essay, however, is to offer some reflections on what he might have meant, for I believe that his words encapsulate a profound solution to what is surely one of the oldest and most fundamental problems of anthropology."[21] And that problem is: what does it mean to say that humans are rational beings distinguished from other species? Because

[21] Tim Ingold, "To Human is a Verb," In Kevin Cahill et al. (Eds.) *Finite But Unbounded: New Approaches in Philosophical Anthropology*, (Boston: De Gruyter, 2017), p. 9. Ingold cites Ramon Lull, a thirteenth-century Christian scholar: "Things, for Ramon Llull, are what they do. For example it is of the essence of fire that it burns. Precisely what fuels the fire, or what is heated by means of it, is an accidental or contingent matter. Perhaps you burn wood to heat water, but neither wood nor water is necessary for there to be fire. What is necessary is that burning should be going on. Likewise, whiteness may whiten this or that body, but there is only whiteness when whitening is going on (Lohr 1992, pp. 29–30). That the existence of a thing or substance is indistinguishable from its activity is not however easily expressed in Latin, and in order to achieve this Llull had to devise new words, modelled on the forms of the Arabic verbs with which he was familiar. One of these neologisms appears when he turns to the problem of defining the human. If what goes for everything else goes for human beings too, then they must likewise be defined by the activity proper to them. Where there are humans, something must be going on. But what? Once again, Llull had to invent a new verb: homificare, 'to humanify'. The human, according to Llull's enigmatic definition, is a humanifying animal: *Homo est animal homificans.* Precisely what human beings do, or how they go about it, is by the way. However wherever and whenever they exist, humanifying is going on. Humans humanify themselves, one another, the animal and vegetable kingdoms, and indeed the entire universe. Thus for Ramon Llull, nearing the end of his long life, as indeed for Ulysses Grant over five centuries later, it seemed that the grammatical form of the human is not that of the subject, whether nominal or pronominal, but that of the verb." Ibid., p. 10.

if we are to see ourselves as verbs and not nouns, meaning as processes and not products, that is a terrain-changing reality for consideration of the thing called intelligence. Because then, the word "intelligent" could no longer be an adjective but an adverb.

Further, from the above cue of the human as nothing but a verb, an irrepressible coming-to-be, we also derive another related angle for our exploration.

> Since all human life is happening, so all creation is occasional: a moment-to-moment improvisation. Whereas God created the world in a single act, and finished the job, "man", wrote Ortega, "makes himself in the light of circumstance, ... he is a God as occasion offers, a 'secondhand God'" (Ortega y Gasset 1961, p. 206). And it is precisely in this task of secondhand creation that imagination comes into play. God needs no imagination, since His creation is already all in place before the act begins. But worldly, mortal humans can only recreate piecemeal, a bit at a time. Recall that in Wieman's definition, 'to do' is to act upon an idea that is already settled within the imagination. The intention or design is there before the act. 'To undergo', by contrast, is to move upstream, to where ideas have yet to crystallise out from the flow of action. As a creative good, the power of the imagination is not one of mental representation, nor is it a capacity to construct images in advance of their material enactment. It is rather the generative impulse of a life that continually runs ahead of itself. Following Ortega, we could say that imagination is another word for the aspiration of not-yet-being. As such, it leads from the front rather than pressing from behind. But where it leads is not yet plotted out before the act begins. As we say colloquially, the propensity of the imagination is to 'roam', to cast about for a way ahead or to improvise a passage; it is not to map final outcomes and all the steps to reach them. And for Ortega, without imagination—without this capacity to run ahead of ourselves—human life would be impossible.[22]

Human existence is creative improvisation involving an imagination that constantly runs ahead of itself. If we nominate this act of creative imagination as intelligence that leads from the front, rather than pushing from behind in accordance with some pre-given plan, then that puts paid to any comparison between organic intelligence and AI which is algorithmic.

But then this view of intelligence presents us with the problem of communication that needs to be kept in perspective, for after all, we have to

[22] Ibid., pp. 16–17.

connect our project to education. And if we take a step into the open, we also ought to be able to step back and reconnect to the pedagogic implications of the novel direction we take.

> According to the normative canon of Western pedagogy, the provision of cultural content to young minds equipped by nature with the capacities to receive it. As such, it is a process of humanisation. A variant etymology, however, traces the word to *educere*, from *ex* (out) plus *ducere* (to lead). In this sense, education is a matter of leading novices out into the world rather than—as it is more conventionally understood—of instilling knowledge in to their minds. To be thus led out is to be both impelled and drawn into the unknown. Education, in this second sense, is not what a person receives in order that they may then go on to do this or that in accordance with existing social or moral precepts. It is rather what the person undergoes: a process not of humanisation but of humanifying. It might perhaps be compared to going out for a walk. In a brilliant meditation on the subject of walking and education, the philosopher Jan Masschelein (2010a, b) argues that walking is not about taking up a standpoint on things. It does not place us in a position, or afford us a perspective, on the basis of which we can then proceed to act. On the contrary, walking continually pulls us away from any standpoint—from any position or perspective we might adopt. "Walking", as Masschelein explains, "is about putting this position at stake; it is about ex-position, about being out-of-position" (2010a, p. 276). Or in a word, it is a practice of exposure. And this is precisely what is achieved by education in the sense of exduction.[23]

From the above, intelligent education would imply constantly pulling away from established viewpoints to new perspectives where we can be out-of-position in a practice of continual exposure. Walking indicates a kind of cosmic meandering that unsettles previously held positions such that the off-setting allows new light of surprise. Thus we are able to connect in education the two sides of the problem—the modes of intellection and of communication, both of which will be further addressed in the next chapter. But ex-position, or an intelligence awakened by means of walking away from established positions, must also assume something that we refer to as intuition. For in walking away, we might simply fall off a precipice. So, even if intelligent becoming runs ahead of itself, as we saw earlier, it cannot be a random walk, but must include an implicit sense of

[23] Ibid.

meaningful direction. Organic life and sentient intelligence are often accompanied by the sending out of "feelers"—intuitive avant-garde—into the field of the real, well before rational intellection processes enter into the act. Further, since not too much is formally known about intuition, we cannot say anything definitively about its unitary or collective status.

The problem of attempting to intellectualize intuition is that it is akin to one of two parallel lines attempting to cross the other. From what little we know and understand of the intuitive process, it runs independent of intellection, and probably for a good reason. And it is something which we need necessarily to include in our discussion because it seems to lead organic or sentience intelligence from the front. Jung's comments about intuition exploring the unknown, and sensing possibilities that may not be readily apparent are most appropriate. What we can definitely say is that intelligence consists of both intellection and intuition, or ingenuity and intuition as Alfred Turing had thought, and as we shall see a few lines later. But sending intuitive feelers into the unknown can feed the senses directly with the possibilities arising therefrom which can be tested later by the intellect.

> The majority of researchers agree that intuition predominantly operates implicitly, without cognitive control and awareness. Nevertheless, other characteristics of intuitive processes (for example, complexity, time, and metacognition) are disputable and depend on the phenomenon studied. We decided to define intuition as the ability to implicitly learn and detect cognitive patterns, and to subconsciously combine information in complex ways to make correct judgments based on fragmentary cues. Intuition is based on various cognitive processes and mechanisms. One of the most fundamental and evolutionarily old of these is the ability to spontaneously acquire complex patterns on the basis of the procedural memory (i.e., implicit learning; Reber, 1993). For example, Reber (1967, 1993) showed that people can unintentionally learn artificial complex grammars (in the Artificial Grammar Learning task; AGL). Despite an absence of explicit knowledge about the rules, participants performed above the chance level (recognizing items as compatible vs. incompatible with a specific grammar), indicating the existence of implicit learning. Evidence for implicit learning has also been provided using different paradigms, for example, detecting hidden covariations (Lewicki, 1986; Lewicki, Hill, & Czyzewska, 1992) and by using the Serial Reaction Time task (SRT, Kaufman et al., 2010). Furthermore, intuitive abilities are likely to govern the integration of cues into a whole in a complex way, without aware access to this process. Individuals can correctly recognize

> things based on little information (Westcott, 1968a), or even subconsciously combine them in order to find new solutions.[24]

Implicit learning is embodied learning, something that cannot be copied as it is not algorithmic in nature. It is not algorithmic as it is not subject to logical control but involves the integration of cues in wholly novel ways without prior awareness or access to the process. To put it differently, there is no programmer behind this cognitive capacity. Algorithms cannot access this process or duplicate it as its ontology is wholly alien to this paradigm. But what is this ontology?

Given where we are in the discussion, this might be a good juncture to turn toward algorithmic processes and ask about the nature of the algorithm and its ontology to begin a differential analysis. Let us begin in that direction by recalling some basic historical facts about the origin of the ideas behind Artificial Intelligence.

> In his 1938 PhD thesis, Turing hoped that formal systems might be extended by including additional rules (then sets of rules, and sets of sets of rules) that could handle the "Gödel problem." He discovered, rather, that the new, more powerful system would have a new, more complicated Gödel problem. There was no way around Gödel's incompleteness. Buried in the complexities of Turing's discussion of formal systems, however, is an odd suggestion, relevant to the possibility of AI. Perhaps the faculty of intuition cannot be reduced to an algorithm, to the rules of a system. But Turing wanted to find a way out of Gödel's limiting result in his 1938 thesis, but he discovered that this was impossible. Instead, he switched gears, exploring how, as he put it, to "greatly reduce" the requirement of human intuition when doing calculations. His thesis considered the powers of ingenuity, by creating ever more complicated systems of rules. (Ingenuity, it turned out, could become universal—there are machines that can take as input other machines, and thus run all the machines that can be built. This insight, technically a universal Turing machine and not a simple Turing machine, was to become the digital computer.) But in his formal work on computing, Turing had (perhaps inadvertently) let the cat out of the bag. By allowing for intuition as distinct from and outside of the operations of a purely formal system like a computer, Turing in effect suggested that there may be differences between computer programs that do math and mathematicians.[25]

[24] Ibid.

[25] Erik J. Larson, *The Myth of Artificial Intelligence* (Cambridge, Massachusetts: Harvard University Press, 2021), p. 8. "Gödel, too, was thinking about mechanical intelligence. Like

Alfred Turing who is largely acknowledged as one of the founding intellectuals behind the idea of the computer had published a paper on the meaning of the word computer. In his paper of 1936, Turing attempted to replace human computational abilities with the idea of a machine doing the same work. He was essentially attempting to eliminate the human factor, which we might sometimes call intuition, in problem solving, and trying to show that any external help or human intelligence was unnecessary. But in attempting to do this he came up against the mathematical genius of Kurt Gödel who had earlier shown that all formal systems were incomplete. In other words, there are propositions that we intuitively know to be true within a system, but which could not be proven to be so within the system. The Incompleteness Theorem, as Gödel's theorem was called, indicated that Turing's project to equate organic intelligence with machinic ones was based on a false premise (of completeness). Turing acknowledged the difficulty, but tried to work around it by proposing the notion of "Ingenuity." The idea was that the factor of intuition could be minimized or even eliminated by using machines serially in which the output of one would be taken as the input of another, and so on, creating increasingly sophisticated systems of rules. Turing wrote: "Mathematical reasoning may be regarded rather schematically as the exercise of a combination of two faculties, which we may call intuition and ingenuity. The activity of the intuition consists in making spontaneous judgments which are not the result of conscious trains of reasoning. These judgments are

Turing, he was obsessed with the distinction between ingenuity (mechanics) and intuition (mind). His distinction was essentially the same as Turing's, in different language: proof versus truth (or 'proof-theory' versus 'model-theory' in mathematics lingo). Are the concepts of proof and truth, Gödel wondered, in the end the same? If so, mathematics and even science itself might be understood purely mechanically. Human thinking in this view would be mechanical, too. The concept of AI, though the term remained to be coined, hovered above the question. Is the mind's intuition, its ability to grasp truth and meaning, reducible to a machine, to computation? This was Gödel's question. In answering it, he ran into a snag that would soon make him world-famous. In 1931, Gödel published two theorems of mathematical logic known as his incompleteness theorems. In them, he demonstrated the inherent limitations of all formal mathematical systems. It was a brilliant stroke. Gödel showed unmistakably that mathematics—*all* of mathematics, with certain straightforward assumptions—is, strictly speaking, not mechanical or 'formalizable.' More specifically, Gödel proved that there must exist some statements in any formal (mathematical or computational) system that are True, with capital-T standing, yet not provable in the system itself using any of its rules. The True statement can be recognized by a human mind, but is (provably) not provable by the system it's formulated in." Ibid., p. 16.

often but by no means invariably correct (leaving aside the question as to what is meant by "correct"). Often it is possible to find some other way of verifying the correctness of an intuitive judgment. One may for instance judge that all positive integers are uniquely factorable into primes; a detailed mathematical argument leads to the same result. It will also involve intuitive judgments, but they will be ones less open to criticism than the original judgment about factorization. I shall not attempt to explain this idea of "intuition" any more explicitly."[26] Although in proposing this, Turing had in effect acknowledged that there existed something called intuition that could not be formalized, nevertheless, the foundations of a technofantasy had been laid. The point we have to address is why this technofantasy might be problematic, especially for education.

> The AI culture has simplified ideas about people, while expanding ideas about technology. This began with AI's founder, Alan Turing, and involved understandable but unfortunate simplifications I call "intelligence errors." Initial errors were magnified into an ideology by Turing's friend and statistician, I. J. Good, who introduced the idea of "ultraintelligence" as the predictable result once human-level AI had been achieved. Between Turing and Good, we see the modern myth of AI take shape. Its development has landed us in an era of what I call technological kitsch—cheap imitations of deeper ideas that cut off intelligent engagement and weaken our culture. Kitsch tells us how to think and how to feel. The purveyors of kitsch benefit, while the consumers of kitsch experience a loss. They—we—end up in a shallow world.[27]

The fact that Turing turned away from the problem of intuition and toward ingenuity or mechanical compensation put a closure on an important distinction. Inquiry into this distinction might have maintained a vital uncertainty around these questions and brought about further debate. But things were changing rapidly—World War II was beginning—and a different world order was in the offing. In times of war or other great social uncertainty, technological pragmatism is the ringside view and everything else takes a back seat. The War put a huge question mark against ideological humanism and humanistic civilization, making people look at machines in a new way. A post-war era of "technological kitsch" would emerge in which elements of a new myth could be found.

[26] Ibid., p. 11.
[27] Ibid., p. 3.

> The scientific part of the myth assumes that we need only keep "chipping away" at the challenge of general intelligence by making progress on narrow feats of intelligence, like playing games or recognizing images. This is a profound mistake: success on narrow applications gets us not one step closer to general intelligence. The inferences that systems require for general intelligence—to read a newspaper, or hold a basic conversation, or become a helpmeet like Rosie the Robot in *The Jetsons*—cannot be programmed, learned, or engineered with our current knowledge of AI. As we successfully apply simpler, narrow versions of intelligence that benefit from faster computers and lots of data, we are not making incremental progress, but rather picking low-hanging fruit. The jump to general "common sense" is completely different, and there's no known path from the one to the other. No algorithm exists for general intelligence. And we have good reason to be skeptical that such an algorithm will emerge through further efforts on deep learning systems or any other approach popular today. [On the cultural side] a healthy culture for innovation emphasizes exploring unknowns, not hyping extensions of existing methods—especially when these methods have been shown to be in adequate to take us much further. Mythology about inevitable success in AI tends to extinguish the very culture of invention necessary for real progress—with or without human-level AI. The myth also encourages resignation to the creep of a machine-land, where genuine invention is sidelined in favor of futuristic talk advocating current approaches, often from entrenched interests.[28]

There are two distinct parts of this new myth or technofantasy—one is scientific and the other cultural. The scientific myth, started by AI founder Turing (although the term was not yet invented), was that ingenuity would ultimately overcome the problem of limits, and specific intelligences would be integrated into general intelligence. This is of course pure fantasy, and even today, after decades of work there is no known path that leads from narrow applications to general intelligence, for general intelligence is not a sum of special applications. As to why that might be the case would be discussed in subsequent chapters. And yet, the public is fed on the idea that actualizing such a possibility is a matter of time. This brings us to the cultural side of the myth. First, not a small part of this is played by entrenched interests including research funding and business promotions. Second, in some strange way, in modern societies obsessed with ease of life and creature comforts, people seem to want to believe that algorithms can do just as well in bringing to them cheap imitations of the good

[28] Ibid., p. 2.

life. And third, not too many are interested in thinking about what exactly are algorithms and what is it that they do, a vital element of public understanding that will set out for them the important distinctions giving self-understanding.

> In philosophy, there has been some interest in algorithms as they relate to cognition, particularly in the philosophy of mind, but few have shown an interest in the algorithm per se. Neither do computer scientists have a well-established idea of the ontological status of their main material of programming, and the lack of consensus on this issue has been noted by prominent computer science publications. Robin Hill has given a definition of algorithm that, though not undisputed, serves to clarify the concept of algorithmic intelligence: "an algorithm is a finite, abstract, effective, compound control structure, imperatively given, accomplishing a given purpose." It is finite in the sense that it allows representations to be articulated in finite time and space, and it is an abstract. We can talk about an algorithm independently of its specific instances; it is not situated in space and time. By effective, Hill means to say that the algorithm is wholly determined, producing the exact same results given the same circumstances. That means that the causal powers of the physical structure instantiating it can be predicted on the basis of what we know about the abstract algorithm: the problem solving abilities, or intelligence, of the algorithm is equal to that of its realizer. Since no additional problem solving powers can be attributed to the physical instantiation itself, it makes sense to also ascribe the abstract algorithm itself the same property of intelligence. Control emphasizes that an algorithm brings about a change from one state to another, and structure reminds us that an algorithm consists of smaller units: the ordered procedural steps of the function. Imperative means that an algorithm is a prescription, which tells how-to. Finally, that it accomplishes a given purpose should make the reader pause at this moment. Was it not claimed in the previous paragraph that an algorithm can have no goal? The key word here is of course "given". The algorithm itself cares not a bit about whether it is performing successfully. It may perform the biddings blindly given by nature, or for a purpose given intentionally by a human scientist, but whenever we talk about whose purpose it is, it is either the system(s) in which the algorithm is being performed, or an external agent.[29]

An algorithm has no goal outside of the specific task it was designed to do, nor can it evaluate its purpose. In that sense, it is a "blind" act that

[29] Even Oygarden, *What is Intelligence?* (Agder: University of Agder, 2019), p. 78.

cannot assess the integrity of the performance. That is to say, its "goal" is external to itself set by someone or something beyond the algorithm. This alone is sufficient to set it apart from sentient intelligence. For the latter is nothing if not a constant seeking of a reality-becoming beyond itself. It may be argued that a natural phenomenon like photosynthesis, although an organic process, also has no goal outside of itself. But nature does not evince photosynthetic activity in isolation, but within a larger purpose. We can of course break it down and isolate the process from the whole it was part of, but it is hardly the original thing. How important is this distinction between intrinsic and extrinsic goals going to be in our understanding of sentient intelligence vis-à-vis AI?

> There are several different reasons why an algorithm does not have a goal in the same sense as a system. First, a system is informed of the states of its parts and therefore acts to maintain its integrity. An algorithm, being a function, is not informed of its functional structure; *it is not even in the loosest kind of sense aware of itself.* Therefore it cannot affect itself, or any self-related goals in an intelligent way. Even if the algorithm could somehow know its own structure, it is fully determined. According to determinism, the same could be said of a system, but in that case, a system is not determined by its own formal structure, but by the physical world. What reasons are we then left with to say that there is such a thing as algorithmic intelligence? It turns out that algorithms by themselves have enormous capacity for complex problem solving, and capable of feats of intelligence that we do not need to describe in terms of knowledge, goals, or understanding. The accomplishments of AI-algorithms left to their own devices in recent years have been stunning, at times solving problems far more efficiently than entities we do not hesitate to label as intelligent. Still, precisely because knowledge or understanding play no fundamental part in the programs, they are often dismissed as not really intelligent, despite clearly satisfying the criteria of capacity for complex problem solving. My view is that we should acknowledge that algorithmic intelligence is real, impactful, but very different. This very basic concept of intelligence refers to both abstract functions or algorithms that when physically realized would be able to solve complex problems, and their physical instantiations. The abstract functions carry an inherent potential of intelligence, and the physical structure performing the function, for instance a set of neurons, are concrete objects with the property of algorithmic intelligence and causal power. The reasons why this has become a subject for debate are the results of AI-research, and in order to understand its potential

significance, we must examine the radically different approach to (artificial) intelligence that machine learning represents.[30]

The key ontological point above is that an algorithm is fully determined, even when it demonstrates remarkable problem-solving capacities. But what is missed in the encomium to machinic problem-solving capacity is that someone needs to find, discover, or set up problems that need to be solved, as well as invent the paths to solving them. And for this one requires knowledge of the real world as well as understanding of contextual relations, neither of which play any role in the algorithmic environment. Besides, the very types of logic used by sentient intelligence and algorithmic approach are distinct: "The Problem of Inference involves thinking, in other words, that which will work for human-level AI (or anything even close to it) is the one we don't have a clue how to program or engineer. The problem of inference goes to the heart of the AI debate because it deals directly with intelligence, in people or machines. Our knowledge of the various types of inference dates back to Aristotle and other ancient Greeks, and has been developed in the fields of logic and mathematics. Inference is already described using formal, symbolic systems like computer programs, so a very clear view of the project of engineering intelligence can be gained by exploring inference. There are three types. Classic AI explored one (deduction), modern AI explores another (induction). The third type (abduction) makes for general intelligence, and, surprise, no one is working on it—at all. Finally, since each type of inference is distinct—meaning, one type cannot be reduced to another—we know that failure to build AI systems using the type of inference undergirding general intelligence (abduction) will result in failure to make progress toward artificial general intelligence, or AGI."[31] Abduction is a kind of logical inference that works by drawing analogies between different elements or situations. In other words, abduction is metaphoric and hugely cultural, for it is through culture that we develop the progressively complex inner life from where analogies are drawn. Much of human communication is metaphoric, and works through nuanced references to parallel or historical events that are never made explicit, and the human receiver being part of the culture knows the allusion being made. The

[30] Ibid., p. 79.
[31] Ibid., p. 4.

machine has no inner life and hence no cultural pool from which to draw analogies.

And that brings us to the final element in the current AI environment that needs attention and that concerns something that is called Machine Learning.

> Machine learning is the study of algorithms that improve through experience. In other words, they learn. Machine learning goes by different names: pattern recognition, statistical modelling, data mining, knowledge discovery, predictive analytics, data science, adaptive systems, self-organizing systems etc. Learning algorithms, algorithms that produce new algorithms, are the inverse of programming, where the task is finding the best algorithm for producing the desired output. Pedro Domingos describes machine learning as "the scientific method on steroids". It follows the same process of generating, testing, and discarding or refining hypotheses, but in a fraction of the time it would take a human scientist. This is the reason these algorithms are called learners. Their task is not to perform operations entirely predicted and instructed by their human creators, but learning itself. Today, just a few algorithms are responsible for the great majority of machine-learning applications. Naïve Bayes is one, the "nearest-neighbour" algorithm another. They are all much simpler than the algorithms they replace, which are explicit instructions in how to go about solving the problems in the way a human would. This leads Pedro Domingos, among others, to speak about the "master algorithm", a single, universal-purpose learning agent. The thesis is that all knowledge—past, present and future—can be derived from data by a single, universal learning algorithm. Inventing such an algorithm, Domingos says, would be one of the greatest scientific achievements of all time, and the last thing we will ever have to invent, because it will from then on invent for us. In The Master Algorithm, Domingos divides the current research landscape into what he calls the five tribes of machine learning: the symbolists, the connectionists, the evolutionaries, the Bayesians and the analogizers. Among them, different theories of intelligence are represented, each with different lines of arguments for, or sometimes against, the existence of a master algorithm. When investigating the nature of algorithmic intelligence, these are the approaches currently available to explore.[32]

Machine learning is the most advanced kind of algorithm in the AI environment that "learns through experience." But what does experience, especially learning through experience, mean? This question will be

[32] Ibid., p. 81.

addressed in Chap. 4. But meanwhile, the machine learning proponent's ambition or dream is to formulate a master algorithm, a single universal-purpose learning agent that will make redundant many of the specific applications oriented algorithms. The idea is that a single learning algorithm can derive all knowledge from available data since all are connected by means of common underlying logical processes. Besides, the dream is that "it is the last thing we will have to invent," for from then on it will do the inventing for us. Of course, the primary mix-up here is between data-knowledge and invention-knowledge. The two are of different logical types, and there is not a shred of evidence at hand to show that there might be an equivalence or crossover between the two. In other words, knowledge of the past cannot necessarily and prospectively invent the future, even though we might retrospectively or with hindsight connect or draw a line to the past. But let us look into this matter a little bit more in terms of the variances within AI advocacy.

> Some view algorithmic intelligence as most importantly the ability to manipulate symbols, which means that some kind of external knowledge has to be introduced to the algorithm. Others view the algorithms of the human brain as exactly the kind of algorithm any intelligent system needs, and seek to replicate this through methods of backpropagation in neural networks. Yet others seem to favour the idea that algorithmic intelligence is much more widespread and fundamental in nature, and that it is the force of natural selection we need to apply to cultivate the right kinds of algorithms. Some are more specific in their claims, suggesting that intelligent algorithms essentially are structures that revise beliefs, or that intelligent algorithms deal with synthesising sensory input into conceptual categories. We can differentiate between a strong and a weaker claim of algorithmic intelligence. In the idea of the master algorithm lies the strong claim that algorithmic intelligence is capable of, and in fact responsible for, anything any intelligence can do. The weaker claim is that algorithmic intelligence is a basic abstract form of intelligence that performs some part in any intelligent process, and by itself is capable of much, but not all, that any other kind of intelligent agent or system can do. The notion of algorithmic intelligence is not only visible behind a seismic shift in artificial intelligence, from top-down knowledge engineering to the bottom-up approach of machine learning, it also seems to be on the horizon in neuropsychology, as researchers delve further into the nitty-gritty details of the brain's cognitive processes. Systems and algorithms are, however, very different subjects. At least until a master algorithm is discovered, we should be precise about whether we are

talking about the capabilities of an abstract algorithm, or the sum of properties of a physical intelligent system.[33]

Replication through backpropagation by means of observing and mimicking neural networks seems to be the preferred move ahead. The vision implicit in this approach is one of robotized humanoids going about their business through optimized systems managed by intelligent algorithms. Whether such a vision prima facie elicits alarm, smugness, or downright dismissal depends on our view of the world and our relationship with reality. The problem of course is not with AI per se, but with the creation of an atmosphere wherein *techne* begins to predominate over *poiesis*. The latter is a movement from the Unknown to the Unknowable—no one knows the purpose of evolution; whereas the former is a movement from the known to the knowable—since there is a determined purpose. This distinction cannot be downplayed, but rather needs to be highlighted in order not to allow the AI enthusiasts to destroy human potentiality. The potentialities of an organically intelligent system cannot be reduced to a synchronic sum of properties simply because the very process of organic evolution is diachronic. We can say that intelligent systems are Janus-faced, simultaneously looking in contrary temporal directions. They are also simultaneously data-driven and non-informational: we choose to take in information when we want, and refuse information when we do not feel we need to know more. Besides, there is a concerted attempt to make people think that the most pressing problems of the world can be solved by fast processors, whereas the real problems are conduct-based and not based on the paucity of information or of the capacity to process these.

Artificial intelligence (AI) is heralding what is increasingly discussed as the Fourth Industrial Revolution, turning on the extraction and exploitation of data for 'smart' governance through 'data-driven' strategies. AI, or 'the theory and development of computer systems able to perform tasks normally requiring human intelligence' (Jobin et al, 2019, p. 389), is also presented as having the capacity to solve some of the world's most pressing problems across domains such as health, finance, housing, transport, and education. The technology has attracted increased interest given its high-profile successes in simulations, games, smart city operating systems, and self-driving vehicles. A range of approaches to AI such as machine learning, deep learning, and artificial neural networks have framed how data processing

[33] Ibid., pp. 91–92.

> and analysis are now being conducted. Proponents have claimed that commercial applications of AI in society often have a positive social impact by increasing the availability and accessibility of information, a result of more efficient search tools and language-translation tools, provision of better information communication services, optimised transportation systems, and personalised healthcare and education. Current debates have been focusing on AI in education, particularly how the AI ecosystem might be harnessed to progress global education given the need to move teaching and learning online because of the COVID-19 pandemic. As a result, several AI-branded products have begun competing with each other for a place in education. Intelligent assistants, for instance, have been touted as having the capacity to take on the more mundane administrative responsibilities of teachers, such as tracking attendance, and developing lesson plans and classroom activities, thereby freeing up teachers' time to do other things (UNESCO, 2021; Baker et al, 2019). As a consequence of the pandemic, companies around the world have scrambled to gain entry into a lucrative educational technology opportunity, spurring calls and demand for AI in education as a solution to accessible remote learning. While there are increasing cautions around the uses of AI in education (Holmes et al., 2021), the popular media and a range of online spaces representing AI in education stakeholders show widespread acceptance that AI is the future of education.[34]

It seems that AI makes its entry into education by reducing the latter into a system of tasks to be accomplished, and thereafter demonstrating how "intelligent assistants" can reduce the task load of teachers, leaving them free to do more important things. However, it is questionable as to whether teacher work can be fragmented and cut up into convenient packages that are separately identifiable as this or that task. Many would argue that teacher work is made up of unique forms of continuities and gestalts. And therefore, the question we have to ask is whether human or organic intelligence in general should be perceived in terms of performance of tasks. For it may be argued that intelligence is best evinced where no tasks are involved such as in loving, or caring, or nurturing, or in having a quiet moment by oneself, or in looking at a painting, or in suffering a bereavement, or in discussing an idea, or in reading poetry, or in extending a hand in help, or in walking through the woods, or in having thoughts about

[34] Selena Nemorin, Andreas Vlachidis, Hayford M. Ayerakwa & Andriotis Panagiotis (2022): AI hyped? A horizon scan of discourse on artificial intelligence in education (AIED) and development, *Learning, Media and Technology*, DOI: https://doi.org/10.1080/17439884.2022.2095568.

one's finitude, or in seeking or establishing peace, or in turning inwardly toward being, and so on. In evolutionary terms, the tasks before the species have taken different shapes in accordance with a range of imperatives, some environmental and some constructed. The complex trappings and clutter of civilization have grown out of these imperatives and the associated tasks that evolved out of them. AI is one more (algorithmic) task among tasks and also a super or meta task. But the important pedagogic question is not whether AI can carry out all tasks (*techne*) with human efficiency, but whether the non-task domains of sentient intelligence can be shielded from the glare of *techne*. The danger of this blinding glare is that we may be caught like deer in headlights, and become oblivious or indifferent to the side of existence that deals with *poiesis* or truly creative or innovative ways of living. This is the pedagogic imperative that has to counter the technocentric narcissism involving grand narratives of a master algorithm. We are not here to set up a competition between sentient intelligence and AI but to mark out the radical difference in terrain governed by their respective ontologies. This is part of our task in the book. The other part of the task is to use this distinction to highlight our pedagogic responsibility to bring out the potentialities of organic intelligence and the modes of actualizing them. It is only in so doing that we can resist being dominated by the cheerleaders of an increasingly robotized society.

But what shall we do with the myth promoted by AI enthusiasts that true AI is just round the corner, for that kind of talk is increasingly dominant, especially in the corridors of higher education. A way must be found to critically engage with it.

> The myth is not that true AI is possible. The myth of artificial intelligence is that its arrival is inevitable, and only a matter of time—that we have already embarked on the path that will lead to human-level AI, and then superintelligence. We have not. The path exists only in our imaginations. Yet the inevitability of AI is so ingrained in popular discussion—promoted by media pundits, thought leaders like Elon Musk, and even many AI scientists (though certainly not all)—that arguing against it is often taken as a form of Luddism, or at the very least a shortsighted view of the future of technology and a dangerous failure to prepare for a world of intelligent machines. But as I will show, the science of AI has uncovered a very large mystery at the heart of intelligence, which no one currently has a clue how to solve. Proponents of AI have huge incentives to minimize its known limitations. After all, AI is big business, and it's increasingly dominant in culture. Yet the possibilities for future AI systems are limited by what we currently know

> about the nature of intelligence, whether we like it or not. And here we should say it directly: all evidence suggests that human and machine intelligence are radically different. The myth of AI insists that the differences are only temporary, and that more powerful systems will eventually erase them. Futurists like Ray Kurzweil and philosopher Nick Bostrom, prominent purveyors of the myth, talk not only as if human-level AI were inevitable, but as if, soon after its arrival, superintelligent machines would leave us far behind.[35]

The above passage is an important one showing us what we are up against. There is an air of superiority that surrounds the AI talk and the proponents of AI. But not all of us are either seduced or fooled by it. There is a great mystery at the heart of intelligence that intelligence itself is unable to grasp. We know this, the ancients knew this, and now even research says this. But public understanding is misled by lack of proper debate and the attraction for kitsch. Our job as educators is to acknowledge this problem even as we deal with ground realities and work toward the realization of potentiality of the sentient.

Sometimes this latency or potentiality is spoken of in terms of a transcendental or occult capacity to connect to a larger or more intense reality (i.e., make sense of it), or to look beyond everyday constructs. Our transient and ephemeral existence raises all sorts of doubts in susceptible minds as well as those who are unwilling to be fooled by public continuities. The experience of discontinuity makes some wonder if there is such a thing as eternity, not in the sense of continuous and endless time, but in the sense of a timelessness that might end suffering. In our quest for intelligence, we cannot afford to overlook or dismiss such inquiries. Further, since the latter form of queries often refer to arcane texts or experiences, we may need to engage with them perfunctorily, getting out of them what we need for our ontological exegesis. In general, folks who are vocal about spiritual or mystical intelligence approach it in multiple ways and from many directions. Some of this is captured below.

> Marshall and Zohar (2000) also believed that spiritual intelligence is an innate talent which we use it for solving intellectual problems, and put our lives in a wider state of richness and meaning. They defined the characteristics of developed spiritual intelligence as follows:
>
> 1. A high degree of self-awareness.
> 2. Having the capacity of flexibility (active and spontaneous adaptation).

[35] Larson, op. cit., p. 1.

3. Having the capacity of dealing with suffering and its developments.
4. Tend to ask questions of why or how, and search for key answers.
5. Getting inspired of the imaginations and values.
6. The tendency to see the links between different things (being holistic).
7. Unwillingness to injure.
8. Getting away from the context that facilitates unconventional activity (Raghib et al, 2008).[36]

Human life, or sentient life in general, is marked by suffering. In fact, and although we might not like to admit it, thought spends endless hours wallowing in various types of suffering, so much so that one of the most intelligent persons ever to be born to the species, the Buddha, saw suffering (Skt. ***dukhah***) as the principal and endemic condition of human existence. The Buddha therefore proposed that the most intelligent thing human beings can do is to free themselves from suffering. Of course this is a tall order, but he did propose a systematic way of approaching the extinguishment of suffering. Now, machines do not suffer, for they do not have an inner life like the sentient do. We do not know the source of our inner life or the psyche, and therefore cannot create an artificial version of it in the machine. In the Bible, the root of suffering is Original Sin, or non-divine-sanctioned knowledge, and logically then, the machine itself becomes part of that proscribed knowledge or Sin. Hence, although machines do not and cannot suffer, we have to suffer the machine. An important part of spiritual intelligence is an understanding of suffering and progressive emancipation from it. High degree of flexibility (taking nothing for granted), acute self-awareness, and the capacity to see inherent connections between things, as mentioned in the above passage, are fragments of the pedagogy of spiritual intelligence.

> From the perspective of Woleman, spiritual intelligence is the human capacity for asking questions about the meaning of life and simultaneously experience the connection between each of us and the world in which we live. In his view, spiritual intelligence is composed of seven factors include:
>
> 1. Caring: paying attention to physical processes such as eating, regular meditation, and exercises such as yoga and tai-chi.

[36] Mehdi Golverdi, Spiritual Intelligence: Aspects, Components and Guidelines, *International Journal of Management, Accounting and Economics Vol. 1, No. 2*, September, 2014, ISSN 2383-2126 (Online), 1667.

2. Enlightenment: involving of mind in reading spiritual issue, sacred texts and analyzing them.
3. Divinity: the sense of connection with God, a higher power, and with a source of divine power.
4. Spirituality in childhood: the intellectual interests and activities in childhood such as attending religious ceremony and reading sacred texts by parents.
5. Ultra-sensory perception: the experiences that are referred to supernatural or sixth sense.
6. Psychological trauma: spiritual awareness which are reached by having and transcending painful experiences.
7. Paying attention to community: performing spiritual activities such as donation, or volunteering activities which will be beneficial to the community.[37]

The idea of meditation as a way to free the mind of clutter is a common and popular idea, and is often synonymous with spirituality. But what exactly is meditation and why is it of value to spiritual intelligence? The great rishi Patanjali of ancient India answers this question in his famous work the *Yogasutras*. The very first sutra says that yoga or meditation is the negation of mental chatter (*Yogaschah chittavritti nirodhah*). And what is its value? A decluttered consciousness is freed of the debris of personal delusions and fantasies, giving rise to clarity of vision or intelligence. This transpersonal intelligence is qualitatively different from the ego-based cleverness that we try to duplicate in machines, and opens the door to community values such as caring and goodwill.

Jahani (2010) extract 15 components of spiritual intelligence from his thesis which include the following:

1. Knowing and believing in a divine presence.
2. Making work and life meaningful.
3. Developing deep self-awareness.
4. Gaining spiritual wisdom.
5. Having lofty goals in life and work.
6. The ability to use inspired resources to solve problems in life.

[37] Ibid., p. 168.

7. The capacity for virtuous behavior (forgiveness, charity, humility, gratitude, etc.).
8. Willingness to serve.
9. The ability to align individual and community goals.
10. Having insight, understanding, and diagnostic powers.
11. Work conscience.
12. Systematic thinking (regarding the dimensions of the human spirit).
13. Paying attention to spiritual values.
14. Having positive feelings.
15. The ability to ask fundamental questions and find fundamental answers.[38]

The word I will pick on is Presence. In spirituality, there is the necessity of Presence or the fullness of achieving the present. Agamben has written: "God or the good or the place does not take place, but is the taking-place of the entities, their innermost exteriority. The being-worm of the worm, the being-stone of the stone, is divine. That the world is, that something can appear and have a face, that there is exteriority and non-latency as the determination and the limit of every thing: this is the good. Thus, precisely its being irreparably in the world is what transcends and exposes every worldly entity. Evil, on the other hand, is the reduction of the taking-place of things to a fact like others, the forgetting of the transcendence inherent in the very taking-place of things. With respect to these things, however, the good is not somewhere else; it is simply the point at which they grasp the taking-place proper to them, at which they touch their own non-transcendent matter."[39] We are perennially fleeing from grasping ourselves as we are, and out of that fear we try to create duplicates, our machinic alter egos. Spiritual intelligence is the transcendence that inheres in the "taking-place" of ourselves as we are. Let us next look briefly at the path charted by the subsequent chapters.

Following the Introduction, Chap. 2 is titled "Methods of the Sentient." This chapter delves into the processes and methods of sentient intelligence and the nature of reality production that is involved. Without a minimal grasp of the ontology of intelligence, we are not in a position to assess the artificial or the machinic variety. It will entail going into theory in some detail, and for this we will follow the path laid out by the philosopher Xavier Zubiri. Why Zubiri? The latter's method is in alignment with our

[38] Ibid., p. 169.

[39] Giorgio Agamben, *The Coming Community* (Minnesota: University of Minnesota Press, 1993), p. 14.

purpose as it bypasses the traditional approaches to the metaphysics of cognition such as the conventional split between epistemology and ontology—no such split exists in existential experience, or on the phenomenological plane. Instead, Zubiri begins his inquiry into intellection and intelligence on a fresh philosophical page simply, by asking: What does it mean to know something as distinct from the capacity to register a mechanical correspondence between knower and object? In what does reasoning intelligence consist? What is the method of this knowing? Does knowing things as real mean that we know what they are in actuality or does it merely indicate cognitive cataloging? Or are things beyond apprehension in actuality, which was Kant's position? Contra Kant, Zubiri argues that human intelligence seeks to know what things are in themselves, and not merely record or represent. But this attempt at authentic knowledge is never complete even in an ordinary sense, prompting the shift to additional powers of (scientific) cognition, rather like those who appeal to the occult when ordinary cognitive powers seem insufficient. The first step in sentient knowing is when a whole field of sensations collapse, becoming an object or a thing, rather like the production of a particle. This thingification goes on all the time but at a subliminal level, leaving consciousness free to negotiate the relations between things at a higher level. But in looking into the ontology of intelligence we cannot avoid going into the production level of the object of intelligence.

Central to the organic, sentient intelligence is attitude within which the recuperation of a simulacrum is only one possibility among many, and we must not count any specific construct as more authentic than any other, nor must we allow ourselves to imagine that such a simulation exhausts sentient potentiality. For the capacity of organic intellect to produce reality will always be beyond the reach of any construct. Why so? Sentience must always infinitely recede before what it has produced—the power of Will cannot capture it. We have to understand the temporal and spatial characteristic of an object as a particular actualization within an infinite attitudinal flux that derives its infinitude from the Open reality ground. The function of organic intelligence is to infinitely recede before the reality "dross" it has produced as the material consequence of different actualizations, as will be explained in the pages to come. The civilizational trash including material objects—vehicles, planes, rockets, missiles, structures—as well as non-material objects—ideas, information, data, knowledge, artificial "intelligence"—must be understood as grounded objects, unavoidable spin-offs of the living process rather than anything essential (having any essence). These are dead even before they are produced, and consciousness must infinitely withdraw from it, and not get caught up in the civilizational clutter. It must learn to extricate itself from its self-created refuse. The essential pedagogical task therefore is to unclutter and free up living intelligence so that it can become alert to the process of reality production, an unavoidable part of existence, and yet remain free of it as pure potentiality. By means of an inquiry into the method of intellection we are able to open up a systematic angle into the ontological distinction between organic or sentient intelligence and machinic or artificial cognition. We can see that the latter does not consist of the *experience* of anything because it has no inner life toward truth; it can only proceed along the logical mode of information processing by means of algorithms. But the truth of logic is not the truth of reality, even if it may include a facet of the latter. Only sentient intelligence can experience reality, and this experiencing consists at the very least of four distinct modes, namely, orientation, compenetration, corroboration, and interpellation. All of these are explained in the chapter, laying the foundation for an ontological understanding of intelligence.

Next, Chap. 3 illustrates some highpoints of intelligent thinking, by means of discourse and content analysis, dialogic exchanges between famed scientists, who were beginning to emerge as notable thinkers in their respective fields, in order to better understand the thinking by which they progressed. The breathless power of these dialogues would make it clear to even diehard supporters of AI in education as to why human intelligence has little to do with machinic capacities other than being able to program and use them as glorified computing machines or speedy search engines. It is my submission that toying with AI ideas as though they were somehow approximations of conscious intelligence or are potential replacement for general human intelligence severely detracts from the growth of young minds as critical and creative thinkers independent of AI environment and influence. The work and purpose of the two kinds of capacities are qualitatively different, belonging to two different orders. A compilation of court cases is not a legal argument, a literature review is not a novel, a set of affordances or efficiencies is not the physics problem, an extensive collection of rhythm and meter is not poetry, and so on. One could give countless examples that show why the current hyperbuzz around AI is mere hype, even motivated hype and nothing else, that, if taken seriously, would lead to the immature becoming even more deprived. When the razzmatazz dies down, the folks who will be left holding the pieces will surely be those who had taken the circus for real, with the actual issues being higher gun violence and lower well-being. The awakening to a problem like depression as a phenomenon cannot be digitalized even if its subsequent investigation may involve advanced diagnostics. Attempting to seek digital simulation in intellectual pursuit leads to a sterile mindscape in which the unwary risk being stranded.

The reason for laboring the point here is because too much is being made of AI and machine learning currently, including painting scenarios that connect it to the future of education and even to that of humanity itself. The chapter detects some important differences between the two ontologies—conscious intelligence and artificial intelligence. One is the capacity for problematization, for which genius is necessary. Once a problem is set up, it is relatively easy to work toward a solution, and a variety of tools including AI can be pressed into service to seek it. Each problematization in modern science, including those of Ernst Mach, Niels Bohr, Wolfgang Pauli, Albert Einstein, Werner Heisenberg, Erwin Schrödinger, to name but a few, was a leap of faith into the Unknown, based on learned intuition and extrapolation. No machine intelligence can do this because all algorithms, no matter how sophisticated, come out of past ontologies; only the living can be truly emergent because it is led on by uncertain elicitations and creative sources that are not fully understood. Another difference we find with regard to embodied intelligence is its aporetic relation with the frontiers of the known. What does that signify? The furious debate between scientists about the meaning of the strange behavior of photons/lightwaves as well as the trajectory of electrons is indicative of an aporetic disjunction. The fact that one version—the Schrodinger wave equation—eventually came to be the dominant version does not mitigate this fact. And what is the fact? It is that as each version or theory aims into the dark, their hitting something does not bring total clarity, but only raises more questions. This is very important to understand. AI goes from the known to the known, whereas at the frontiers of knowledge, organic intelligence goes from aporia to aporia, and occasionally produces firm knowledge as a dialectical spin-off.

Next, Chap. 4 looks at the educational consequences of mixing up the different ontological categories—one that possesses inner life and another that does not. Once there is clarity about the ontological difference, there is clarity about the need to differentiate organic or conscious intelligence from material or machinic ones, and put an end to loose, immature talk that brings about an aridness. Education must begin with this clarity.

Rejecting the temporal indefinitude of public time and thereby machinic time, the living intelligence must learn to work in the opposite direction, that is, with the fact of finitude. Its anxiety and desire for transcending finitude must be directed at the discovery of an eternal now independent of time. The first educational lesson therefore is that living intelligence must not use time as a bank account. It must learn to reject fake temporality and deny any significance to finitude or indefinitude. It must believe in duration as distinct from time. This means, while futurism as a social attitude cannot be avoided, we must educate ourselves to live simultaneously on another plane in which the progression of events is seen as nothing but a circus—going around in circles—that has no lasting significance. Therefore, the timeless now is all that we have, and that must be lived fully. The intelligence of the timeless now or of simply being is of no use to the machine, but is of the greatest significance to the sentient. This obviously requires a lot of mature thinking and experimenting, but nevertheless needs to be articulated properly as a part of educational phenomenology.

The second important educational lesson is to resist the confused narrative around the Turing test seriously. The comparison between machine intelligence and human intelligence is based on unutterable ontological confusion and perhaps even a degree of motivated social engineering. As Heidegger has pointed out, to talk of artificial intelligence before there is proper understanding of organic intelligence is to be disoriented and immature. We really have no proper understanding of what or how our consciousness perceives and does things—we only have the end products in view. We may assume that the brain works like a computer which is its own brain-child. But whether the material off-spring is anything like the living original is something about which no one has a clue. What is more, there is no known way to figure out what is going on in the brain simply because logically one would need a superior mind-brain to do that. Hence, putting electrodes in the brain won't do, cutting open dead brains won't do, scanning the structure won't do, because in each case, the part story cannot tell us about how the whole actually works in the living being. A proper recognition of this fact is not an admission of defeat but an acknowledgment of what is tenable.

Chapter 5 consists of a running dialogue between the author and an interlocutor that clarifies many things and heightens intermediate understandings. Some examples/extracts are below:

On experimentation: "Experimentation and advancement cannot happen only on the plane of material transformation. Other kinds of experiments have to go on side-by-side. I find myself stuck with this dense body … have to feed it, clothe it, and one day it simply starts to fall apart. So, what's going on? Should I remain a mute spectator busy only with computation and rocket engines, or should I attempt to find out what is going on with me at the existential level? Will artificial intelligence and public time save me from the meaningless void?"

On IQ: "There can be no fixed measure or method of arriving at a quotient that is always meaningful. You can be part of a high-IQ society such as Mensa, and yet act like an imbecile in other areas of life. There is absolutely no guarantee that solving artificial logical problems on a screen or a sheet of paper has anything to do with the phenomenology of lived situations, or that it prepares one to act intelligently in world relations.

On reality: "It all depends on what you mean by "real." If reality is defined by what can be arrived at step by step, then it certainly measures abilities to draw deductions, say, from axioms. But there are no inner steps to creative sensibility, or to love, or to fear, or anxiety, or even the capacity to manage complex human situations. There are no inner steps to intuition, and some of the most valuable exegeses of experience come from the sharpness of insight.

On emotions: "A: Organic intelligence, on the other hand, is in search of surprise and its ground, that is, a break in the pattern that will unfold another level in evolution. We are mostly emotion, and only a fraction, processor. Emotions mostly guide the processing, and not the other way round. Without emotions we are nothing. Processing is a fairly recent thing. Ancient peoples hardly processed, but mainly absorbed whole patterns, resonated with the outside that guided them—the cosmic, that is."

On experience: "Both natural language and mathematical language are not primary. What is primary is experience, which is non-verbal. Education ought to focus on experience, that's all. AI does not have the experience of loving or nurturing or feeling lost; it can only make selections on the *descriptions* of these activities. But the description is never the described."

On consciousness: "Ultimately, intelligence is emergent, not programmed. Look, a baboon or an orangutan cannot be programmed to become a human. It can be made to ape a human or mimic some gestures. But it cannot write *War and Peace*, or understand the *Sermon on the Mount*. No one knows when, or from where anthropic consciousness burst on the scene."

On the psyche: "Intelligence, whether of the organic kind or its analog in the machinic kind, can make hydrogen bombs or thorium engines, space colonies or oceanic ones, but none of these can be accommodated in the psyche. These will always remain as external phenomena. And such being the case, my psyche will remain unresolved by what is going on outside, filled with unknown terrors and anxieties, just like in the millions of generations before us."

On education: "That is where education comes in. Education is the dynamic ground generated by the connection between the psyche and the elemental. It is not something fixed by a curriculum. It is the slow liberation-expansion of the elemental forces guided by ethics. That is why, to be educated is to be unique. One can pick up a trick or two on the side."

On the future: "Having a future or not having a future is not a measure of anything fundamental. Both kitsch and cockroaches have a future. The question is: what is the quality of that future? Is that future headed toward technocratic narcissism or toward ethico-aesthetic emancipation?"

Chapter 6 is about the loss of the space of truth in modernity or loss of poiesis, taken over by techne. This loss results in kitsch replacing the struggle for authentic being. The coming community is both at the edge of destruction through bourgeoisfication, and at the same time at the cusp of a breakthrough beyond petty bourgeois identity. Here then is the crux of the matter—residing in the possibility of a *singularity sans individuality* is the essence of intelligence of the not-public and not-private kind. It is the intelligence of the whatever-being that unites the individual and the collective, that is not symbolic or representational, and that passes from genus to species and back from species to genus, something that Marx had intuited as *Gattungswesen*, a German word often translated as species-being. This singularity, or species-being passing-into-expression, is free of the burden of individuality or personality based identity, thus by-passing the society of kitsch. With the discovery of whatever-being or anonymous identity, the pedagogical ground is laid for the *threptikon* or the nutritive life that eliminates existential deficit. It is also the bridge between being and non-being, which eliminates the fear factor. Taken together, this is the highest form of sentient intelligence in which the latter becomes both the means and the end to species being. In Aristotle, the *threptikon* is the vital power of self-maintenance in the organism ensuring against the tendency of matter to disintegrate. We might call it the binding force of the living organism. But what of the mind-consciousness, what binds it together that can sustain a meaningful psycho-affective response to the world? Of course nothing binds it together, and that is why the individual is often at war with himself, immersed in conflict and self-contradiction in a manner that no machine could ever be.

But just as contradiction is a limiting condition for the psyche, freedom from conflict is an emancipatory condition that is not available to the machinic order. And how is this achieved? There is no positive path to it, for otherwise it would be reduced to the mechanical order. Rather it consists of a negation of properties or characteristics of the social or personal order. One is thereby "freed from the false dilemma that obliges knowledge to choose between the ineffability of the individual and the intelligibility of the universal. The intelligible, according to a beautiful expression of Levi ben Gershon, is neither a universal nor an individual included in a series, but rather singularity insofar as it is whatever-singularity. In this conception, such-and-such being is released from its having this or that property, which identifies it as belonging to this or that set, to this or that class, and it is reclaimed not for another class nor for the simple generic absence of any belonging, but for its *being-such*, for belonging to itself. Thus *being-such*, which remains constantly hidden in the condition of belonging ('there is an *x such that* it belongs to *y*') and which is in no way a real predicate, comes to light itself: The singularity exposed as such is whatever you *want*, that is, lovable."[40] In other words, the *psychic threptikon* is a state of love that is approached through jettisoning all predicates through which conflict, contradiction, and fragmentation arise and are maintained, resulting in a loss of vitality. Hence, the "binding force" of the psyche is nothing other than love freed of civilizational dross. When we place all of these momentous things next to that which is mind-invented, task-based, and simulated, there appears before us not a comparison between two things, but a dimensional difference between them. A rough analogy comes to mind—it is not unlike the juxtaposition of the Buddha or the Christ next to an actor who mimics these characters in front of the crowd or the camera—the authentic placed against the fake. What is required for a pedagogical understanding is the anamnesis, or the coming-to-be of what is. Eros in this context is an implosion that lifts the veil between exteriority and interiority leading to a phenomenological grasp of the fact that simulacra, which appear before us as independent and objectified, are nothing but the exteriorization of mediatized aspects of interiority. The pedagogical task of the coming community or planetary

[40] Agamben, op. cit., p. 1.

humanity is to go beyond mediatization, which also means to set aside all simulacra and artificiality in order to reach for the authentic. The authentic is auto-poietic, and thus it is that we are responsible for giving birth to ourselves, to return to ourselves, not once, not twice, but again and again for attaining our threptic self-nature.

The point of arrival of Western aesthetics is "a metaphysics of the will, that is, of life understood as energy and creative impulse. … And yet what the Greeks meant [by poiesis] was the production of truth and the subsequent opening of a world for man's existence."[41] Therefore it is not surprising that artificial intelligence has acquired this great purchase in the one-dimensional social imaginary during an epoch when the distinction between poiesis and praxis has been forgotten. This loss has enormous philosophical and existential consequences. At one level, it means that the production of the "space of truth" has been replaced and coopted by the production of material substance and task-oriented capabilities, giving rise to the hysterical enthusiasm for simulacra, or that which is fake or inauthentic by definition.

[41] Ibid., p. 72.

CHAPTER 2

Methods of the Sentient

In this chapter we are going to take a long and hard look at this thing we call intelligence, a somewhat lengthy discussion that may border on philosophical exegesis. At this juncture, this is unavoidable, and I seek the reader's indulgence, for ontological misperception can cost us dearly, and we need to set matters straight as far as fundamental distinctions are concerned. It is also a matter of pedagogically fostering the right attitude toward categorical differences. For then we come to understand which paths are ontologically aligned with which, and what are the potentialities, moving forward from there. Here our task will be to grasp the rudiments of the manner in which sentient intelligence comes to posit a world, and also its task therein, as well as the creative risks it must take in positing it. That is to say, we look at the manner in which, out of an immense and incredible range of sensory impingements, we come to delineate a relatively stable reality, and thereafter the susceptibilities that propel us forward to seek a continuous revision of our reality. This relatively stable world is the product of an ethico-aesthetic intelligence, and not an algorithmic-programmable one, simply because the tension between stability and change is an emergent, organic, and embodied dialectic. Only bodies that suffer in the broadest sense of the term, and have an inner life, can possess/develop the embodied intelligence necessary for sentient presence.

K. Roy, *Education, "Artificial" Intelligence, and Cognition*, https://doi.org/10.1007/978-3-031-82263-6_2

We will embark on this exegesis by relying principally on the work of the philosopher Xavier Zubiri of the Madrid School, who, in the words of his translator,

> [R]ejects the traditional view of reality as a zone of things, whether "out there" beyond perception, within the mind, in the realm of ideas, or anywhere else, replacing it with a more fundamental and general notion, that of formality, which refers to the nature of what is present to the intelligence; rejects the traditional four-part division of philosophy into metaphysics, epistemology, logic, and ethics as the primary basis for its organization, instead recognizing that no such strict division has ever been achieved or is even possible, and that a new approach to human intellection is necessary; rejects the traditional notion of God as a reality object, instead conceiving of the suchness as a reality fundament or ground; rejects the traditional idea of reality as "closed" and static, as implied in most conceptions of essence, in favor of a new view of reality and essence as "open"; rejects the agreement of thought and things as the fundamental notion of truth; rejects the traditional notion of sensible intelligence founded on opposition between sensing and intelligence, replacing it with a fully integrated conception: sentient intelligence.[1]

Zubiri rejects the traditional opposition of sensation and intelligence and gives an integrated picture of sentient intelligence. This very different view of human intelligence, whose conditions of emergence are impossible to simulate or emulate by anything outside of the self-nature of this very process itself, is not the process of reasoning but of primordial apprehension. Why is this important for us here? It is because we need an uncompromising and unrelenting view of the process of intelligence that does not allow a simplistic or reductionist understanding to confound the actual process of its emergence.

Let us begin by making a rather deceptively innocuous statement that just as the imitation of anything does not lead to the enhancement of the original, the attempt at synthetic intelligence cannot lead to any qualitative improvement in natural or sentient intelligence. This statement may seem trivial and unnecessary, but then what persuades me to state it here? I do it precisely because we are not talking about artificial vanilla or synthetic vinegar. Intelligence has previously been associated only with

[1] Thomas B. Fowler, "Translator's Introduction," In Xavier Zubiri, *Sentient Intelligence* (Washington D.C.: Zubiri Foundation, 1999), p. vii.

sentient (organo-biological) beings and not with mechanical contraptions or digital processes. That is a recognition of the fact that sentient intelligence is not a copy of anything, but spontaneously begins to seek out its reach and the ground of its activity. The contemporary introduction of this notion of intelligence in association with the non-sentient is quite new and can lead to great ontological confusion as well as psychological upheaval if not treated carefully. At an extreme it could even lead to a sense of cultural despondency and feelings of social redundancy. Hence, we have to distinguish the potential of sentient intelligence from the mere adherence to digital algorithms, however sophisticated, of the simulated.

Following the questions raised in the Introduction, this chapter will inquire into the process of organic intelligence and the nature of sentient seeking. It will involve going into some theory in detail following the path of inquiry laid out by Zubiri, and using a form of analysis that does not split reality along the traditional axes of metaphysics, epistemology, ethics, and so forth. We will go into questions such as: What does it mean to know something as distinct from the capacity to register a mechanical correspondence between observer and observed? In what does sentient intelligence consist? What is the method of this knowing? Does knowing things as real mean that we know what they are in actuality or does it merely indicate cognitive cataloguing? Or are things beyond apprehension in actuality, which was Kant's position? Nevertheless, it is the case here that human intelligence seeks to know what things are in themselves, but this attempt at authentic knowledge seems never complete even in an ordinary sense, prompting the shift to artificial powers of cognition, rather like those who appeal to the occult when ordinary cognitive powers seem insufficient.

According to Zubiri's approach, the first step in sentient knowing is when a whole field of sensations collapse, becoming an object or a thing, rather like the production of a particle. This thingification goes on all the time but at a subliminal level, leaving consciousness free to negotiate the relations between things at a higher level. But in looking into the ontology of intelligence we cannot avoid going into the production of the object of intelligence. This is primordial apprehension that no artificial thing can simulate—the latter can only modify what has already been primordially apprehended by sentient intelligence.

> The object, i.e. the objectual reality, is not an interpretation or anything of the sort; it is the terminus of apprehension. A real thing is a positum, but

> upon the base of in-depth reality; therefore the real thing acquires a character of "ob". That transformation is, then, of categorical order, of categories of actualization. We are not trying to elaborate a representation but to actualize another mode of presentation. For this reason, I repeat, the transformation of a field into a real object is categorical. The real field thing, actualized now as real "in" primordial apprehension, and "re"-actualized in the field manner "among" others and "by" others in the form of affirmation, is now projected upon the base of in-depth reality, upon an ambit actualized in turn as "by", i.e., upon an ambit with the nature of a ground. The "field" of the real thing is open to a "world" in which it is grounded. Then and only then does the real field thing acquire the character of real object.[2]

The world of objects arises each moment through and by means of a perceptual collapse into quantum fields. This may be thought of as the ground of reality that gives rise to actuality. Now what happens when we ignore this fact and instead concentrate on the object or phenomena? Let us take the experience of gravity. Beginning with Newton, we see that the great scientist worked on Kepler's observations about the behavior of planets, asking how or why they managed to stay in their orbits, neither flying apart nor collapsing in a heap. Puzzling over this phenomenon, Newton proposed a force that maintained these celestial objects in their relative positions and called it "gravity." This peculiar effect was present between all bodies in the universe. In general, Newton's law of gravity states that every object in the universe attracts every other object with a force that for any two bodies is proportional to the mass of each object and varies as the inverse square of the distance between them. Every schoolchild knows the equation: $F_g = G(m_1m_2/r^2)$, where m_1 and m_2 are the interacting masses, r is their relative distance vector, and G is generally assumed to be a universal constant found experimentally. However, there is no theoretical or conceptual explanation for the origin of this equation. For instance, why does it have to be "m_1 **x** m_2" and not "$m_1 + m_2$" or m_1/m_2 or something else? No scientist, leave alone any schoolchild, knows the answer to that one. In other words, there is no theoretical or empirical reason why that particular relation should hold rather than another. So while the calculations were correct, they did not provide any explanation. And therein lies part of the mystery, for similar core explanatory gaps exist in other descriptions too including relativistic ones. But let us note that

[2] Xavier Zubiri, *Sentient Intelligence* (Washington D.C.: Zubiri Foundation, 1999), p. 10.

since, for Newton, gravity arises in relation to bodies or masses, these become its efficient cause, and this naïve realism becomes the root of the puzzle of gravity that has not been solved to this day—due mainly to the focus on the object and not the field that produces the object.

What Newton could not possibly see, for its time had not come, is that appearance is not everything. For instance, phenomena may *appear* to be stable (prolonged duration in the same state), but that is not because there is anything inherent in such stability, but because our senses are not calibrated to catch their coming-to-be and ceasing-to-be. The appearance of an object in consciousness is due to the simultaneous collapse of wave fields that leave in their wake remnants of that activity. We come to know that as reality, but its cause remains hidden because the appearance is a conditioned actualization and does not reveal its ground.

> The "ob" is but the actualization of a field thing as a world thing. Only in this actualization is there an "object", i.e., in the rational intellection, in knowledge. That which is intellectively known in primordial apprehension, and that which is intellectively known affirmatively, are not, formally, objects. Only what is intellectively known rationally is an object. This openness of field to world is an openness which leads not to what a field thing already intellectively known "toward" others of the field is, but rather to whatever that intellectively known field thing now is "toward" grounding reality itself. In virtue of this, the transformation of a real thing into objectual reality has precise characteristics: a) It is a transformation not in the mode of representing the real, but in its mode of being present. Objectuality is the terminus of a transformation only of categorical actuality; b) It is a transformation along the lines of the "toward"; the field "toward" is transformed into a "toward" the in-depth. c) This transformation is determined by the real itself, because the "toward" is a mode of reality. The field real in its "toward" is what presents to us that real in its "toward" the in-depth. What is the character of this transformation? The transformation concerns, at one and the same time, intellection and the real thing. With respect to intellection, the transformation does not consist in a change in the act of intellection qua act. It is a transformation which determines, in intellection, something which is less than an act but more than mere capacity. This modalization is just what constitutes actuity. An object is not the terminus of a representation but the terminus of an intellective attitude. The transformation consists, then, intellectively, in the change of act into attitude. The "ob" is intellectively constituted as a terminus of an attitude.[3]

[3] Ibid.

In the above lines we encounter a conceptual move *par extraordinaire*—that move lies in the introduction of the term attitude. In attempting to give us an understanding of the process of actualization of objects, the writer has ontologized the idea of attitude. Going back to the example of gravity, we perceive the phenomenon as such due to an intellective attitude. Because of the attitudinal terminus, we have struggled with the idea of gravity even though there may not be anything like it. Moving on from Newton, we see that in Einstein's General Relativity, the effects of gravitation are ascribed to space-time curvature instead of being attributed to some arbitrary action-at-a-distance. The free-falling objects move along locally straight paths in curved space-time giving them their typical orbital behavior. The degree of curvature of space-time is in turn attributed to the quantity of associated mass present—the greater the mass the more the surrounding curvature. Hence, this too is mass-based thinking in a sense, although a little more abstractly. Besides still being distantly captive to the mass-based paradigm, this also raises the following questions: Why would the presence of mass distort the so-called space-time? Is space-time a 'thing' that is subject to distortion? What is the necessary principle involved here? Does it not disturbingly seem like a projection from the terrestrial experience of weight pressing down upon a surface and distorting it? And so on. In fact, visual explanatory models liberally show heavy balls making dents on tense surfaces, quite innocent of the fact that *they are assuming what needs to be explained*. No convincing answers to these questions have been forthcoming from the followers of relativity theory. So, from Newton's ghostly action-at-a-distance, we arrive at the equally mystical "curvature" of some hypothetical space-time. Nevertheless, General Relativity has experienced considerable success at the descriptive level due to being able to predict phenomena such as precession of Mercury's perihelion, binary pulsars, the red-shift of light, the equivalence principle, and so on. But notwithstanding its descriptive and predictive success, general relativity offers no explanation for the cause of space-time curvature or its relation to mass, and there is no mechanism to describe why gravity works the way it does. Hence, let us note that, paradigmatically speaking, general relativity too depends on causative mass or presence of bodies for the hypothetical space-time curvature. In a sense, it simply begs the question just as Newton's idea of action-at-a-distance did. We can see that although less objectified, relativity theory too relies on a paradigm deeply connected to terrestrial experience, albeit in very different ways than Newton's hypothesis did. And neither theory is able to explain the energy that produces gravitational force. This is the ontological attitude that is referred to above. It is the non-comprehension of ontological attitude that has resulted in confounding the matter of gravity.

However, it is only the sentient, the conscious intelligence, that can spontaneously backtrack and understand the problem with the process of understanding itself, and doubt its own paradigm of thought. It is only the sentient that possesses *ontological attitude* as the basis of knowing and not mere cognitive representation. When we lose the capacity for seeking the reality-ground and reflexivity, sentience begins to resemble the mechanical. The machine has no attitude. Hence, for the human it is not a question of fearing an out-maneuvering of the sentient by the artificial, but the possibility of the sentient being reduced to the mechanical through its worship of simulation and an absence of self-understanding in attitude. Central to the organic, sentient intelligence is attitude within which the recuperation of a simulacrum is only one possibility among many, and we must not count any specific construct as more authentic than any other, nor must we allow ourselves to imagine that such a simulation is beginning to reflect sentient capacities. For the capacity of organic intellect to produce reality will always be beyond the reach of any construct. How so? Sentience will always infinitely recede before what it has produced. We have only to understand the temporal and spatial characteristic of an object as a particular actualization within an infinite attitudinal flux that derives its infinitude from the Open reality ground. The function of organic intelligence is to infinitely recede before the reality "trash" it has produced as the material consequence of different actualizations, as will be explained in the pages to come. The civilizational trash including material objects—vehicles, planes, rockets, missiles, structures—as well as non-material objects—ideas, information, data, knowledge, artificial "intelligence"—must be understood as grounded objects, unavoidable spin-offs of the living process rather than anything essential (having any essence). These are dead even before they are produced, and consciousness must infinitely withdraw from it, and not get caught up in the civilizational clutter. It must learn to extricate itself from its self-created refuse. The essential pedagogical task therefore is to unclutter and free up living intelligence so that it can become alert to the process of reality production, an unavoidable part of existence, and yet remain free of it as pure potentiality.

> That which is actualized in this new attitude, i.e. what is going to be intellectively known rationally, is not the res objecta as objecta, but the res

objecta as res. The “ob” only has the character of referring, and it refers to the reality of which it is actuality. In the intellective attitude the real itself is actualized in “ob”; but it is always an actualization of the real. The transformation, then, falls back upon the actualization in an attitude. Knowledge, I repeat, is not a representation of things, but an actualization of them in that new attitude of the “toward”. In this attitude, the real is objectually projected onto the in-depth base, i.e., it is actualized as worldly reality. This projection, and therefore the knowledge itself, can be of quite varied nature. Knowledge is not just science, nor is it principally science. There are other modes of knowledge, for example poetic knowledge, religious knowledge, etc., just as there are also other known realities which are not things, for example one’s own or someone else’s personal reality. Now, knowledge is not principally theoretic; it is not because it is not radically theoretic. The radical aspect of knowledge is in the attitude of the “toward” determined by the real itself, an attitude in which the real is actualized in an “ob”. The rest is but modalizations of this radical structure. Here then is what objectuality is, and what the attitude which determines the transformation of the real thing into real object is. This objectuality is only a categorical correlate of an attitude, in which the real is actualized in an “ob” by projecting it—and only projecting it—upon the world as an ambit of grounding. This real was previously actualized as “in” and “re”. Therefore its projection upon the ambit of grounding leaves open the intellection of the ground of that objectual reality as a moment of the world.[4]

We experience a stable reality due to the fact that we ourselves are simultaneously being produced and reproduced out of an open field. Thus knowledge of the world is not a re-presentation of what is, but its very production or actualization out of a ground. It is not only the object but the observer who is also projected “toward” a ground and recuperated as such in actuality. Going back to my earlier example on gravity, it would help to understand the phenomenon of “gravity” if we could debunk the notion of masses or bodies or superfluids altogether as nothing but intermediate concepts and not something ontological. This view allows us to be consistent with the so-called Big-Bang which had to be a duality-free moment—*the separation of mass and no-mass or vacuum logically must be a derivative of the originary moment.* As the universe expanded and cooled, there is a corresponding local contraction or compression in order to be true to the conservation principle. Mass is thus no other than this compressional balance. Ourselves as well as other objects are nothing other

[4] Ibid., p. 45.

than compressed nothingness with varying densities. The problem that remained to be explained within this paradigm is the effect these relative densities have on each other that appears to us as "gravity." However, this problem disappears when we discard space/mass distinction, and the so-called gravitational effect may be explained in terms of the effect of a continuum of relative concentrations. In other words, the world is a continuum of dense nothingness and less dense nothingness—vast dense spaces like the stars, and relatively smaller ones like planets, further on till we reach small-sized objects like ourselves. All matter is logically nothing other than densified original nothingness that develops a towardness as evolution. Dense spaces capture smaller densities because around them are dynamic vacuum-like low density spatialities. In this manner of viewing, there is no need to posit anything mysterious like space-time curvature or gravitational force or energy. It is enough to tap into the original unitary moment in which there is no separation, followed by progressive separation between different degrees of concentration. Using the logic of an original moment as the prime basis of our thought experiment, we can see that the observer as well as the observed must have appeared in a complementary manner. As to how a part of that becomes sentient and the other part remains without the towardness will be discussed later. But for now we can say this much that "knowledge is always intrinsically and formally an open problem. It is not sufficient that the field of the real is actualized for us as object. It is actualized for us as object precisely in order for us to intellectively search for its in-depth nature. For that it is necessary that this nature be accessible to intellection. That is the second point of the formal structure of knowing: after the constitution of objectuality, the access to the ground of the real."[5] Returning to our example, successive attempts at explaining the phenomenon of gravity have in actuality confounded the question: Newton's "action-at-a-distance" gave way to Einstein's "space-time curvature," and from thereon to more recent "vortex theory." But in each case unexplained assumptions have remained central to the theories or hypotheses in question. Why? It is because we have not understood this towardness in intellection. Gravity as a phenomenon must be traversed and a beyondness developed. Thus, in rethinking gravity as nothing other than the obverse and inevitable side of cosmic expansion changes the paradigm and eliminates the problem of gravity. The reason we remain stuck on earth is not due to gravity or some other mysterious force, but because

[5] Ibid., p. 67.

we along with other object-masses are nothing other than compressed nothingness ourselves, the inevitable alter side of decompression or universal expansion. All we need is the conservation principle and nothing else to understand this miraculous phenomenon. Instead of proceeding from the mass-end of reality, we need to move from the nothingness end. Progressive expansion of nothingness requires a balancing contraction or densification of nothingness. Vast expanding nothingness is balanced by vast densifications as cosmic expansion progresses. However, *this is a continuum and not a discrete process*, although mass appears as discrete to our sensibilities. The densification is in continuous relation with the surrounding relatively non-densified nothingness. It is these relative nothingnesses that produce the effect of gravity, and not some unique force.

> It is by projecting the field real onto the base of indepth reality, onto the world, that we seek the rational intellection of field things, i.e., their knowledge. Knowledge is search. Let me reiterate that we are not dealing with the search for some intellection, but rather with an intellection which qua intellection is inquiring, which is inquiring itself as a mode of intellection. Since to be an intellection is to be a mere actualization of the real, it follows that the search is an actualization brought to completion in that mode of actualizing which is inquiry. Where does one search for that actualization? We have already seen where: in the world. World is the respectivity of the real qua real. And it is in this sense that it is something beyond the field. The field is respectivity, but it is just sensed respectivity, the sensed world. To go beyond the field is to go from "field" to "world". This world is not, formally, something sought, but something given. The world is given not as something which is there "facing" me; rather, it is given in that mode of reality which is the "toward". It is for this reason that the world is formally something "beyond" the field. In the world thus actualized is where one seeks that which we wish to rationally know intellectively, that which we wish to know.[6]

What seems to be the case is that in an ultimate sense, all intelligence is self-inquiry, or an inquiry into itself. This is a key point here. Organic sentience or natural intelligence spontaneously seeks its own ground. No mechanical intelligence can do that, and even if it could, it can only turn to the algorithm or the program as its author. What drives natural or organic or sentient intelligence toward its ground? It is not the content of

[6] Ibid., p. 73.

consciousness, or the world of objects, that can help sentience toward its goal but a spontaneous passion or Eros. The object world is a mere spin-off of this spontaneous movement toward the ground of being and becoming. Whereas, data (object information) and its analysis is the goal of machinic intelligence, for sentient intelligence the goal is radically different. "What is it that one seeks in the world? One seeks the real considered with respect to the world. Worldly reality is actualized precisely as a "to be grounding". The world is thus the ambit of grounding. And it is just on account of this that the world, that which is beyond the field, is in-depth reality. In-depthness does not consist in any kind of mysterious root, but in being the "for" of the field itself qua worldly. Therefore, that which one seeks in this progression from the field toward the worldly is the ground of the field. Ground, as I have already said many times, is not necessarily a cause, but the mode in which that which is grounding grounds, from itself, the grounded and formally passes into what is grounded. Cause is only a mode of ground. The ground is therefore, ultimately, the world in a real thing. What one seeks is, then, this ground. One does not seek the world, but the ground of the real in the world, transforming the field reality into objectual reality. Neither does one seek an object. World and object are not what is problematic. What is problematic is always just objectual reality qua reality in the world. This problematic business is what one seeks, viz. the ground of this determinate field thing. In virtue of this a question arises: How does one seek that which is sought, that is, the ground of the world?"[7]

The objective world is a fickle place, whose essential character is change. Is there a ground behind this transitoriness, this ephemerality? Behind the patterns in a kaleidoscope there are colored shards and a screen that provides the support for the changing patterns. Is there something similar here that acts as a support for the bringing forth of objects? Further, why is my experience of a tree temporally more stable and extended than a bird in flight, that is to say, less ephemeral, post actualization? Sentient intelligence seeks the ground for each actualization—that is its primary drive. Of course the major question that comes up concerns method. How does the intelligence go about seeking the ground? "This 'how' is strictly and formally an intellective mode. Now, the 'how' of the search for the fundament in the world is what constitutes method. A method is how one forges a way, a way toward the ground. A method is therefore the way of

[7] Ibid., p. 93.

knowing as such. The necessity and nature of the method is not just a type of human necessity. It is that, but this necessity is founded upon an essential moment of reality, upon the constitutive openness of the real, merely in its respectivity. As ambit of respectivity, the world is open; therefore, as a moment of respectivity of each real thing, reality is open in each thing. And the 'how' of the search for the ground is set in this very openness; it is that which transforms the intellective movement into a progression among the real. Method is a way. Neither the world nor the real object is a problem; the problem is the way from the real object to its ground. Thus it is necessary to ask ourselves: what, precisely, is a method? And what is its intrinsic and formal structure? These are the two points which we must examine. Here we ask ourselves in what method consists. We are not interested in what a particular method is; that we shall see later. What we are now interested in is what comprises a method as a moment of rational intellection, i.e., what comprises the methodic moment of reason."[8] But what is a method? The method discussed here is not a specific method or even a human method but is founded upon the very constitutive nature of the real. In other words, it is not characterized by anthropological closure, but is an ontological potential that is open—each thing in its objectification contains this openness as a potential to move forward toward the ground. The possibility of gaining proximity to the ground resides in the very manner of construction and progression in the real field. Thus the method of sentient intelligence needs proper investigation and further clarification.

> 'Method' is not synonymous with what is usually called the 'scientific method'. To be scientific is but a possible modalization of what it is to be a method. Method is something more radical; it is the way of access. The concept of "way" or "path", *hodos*, was probably introduced into philosophy by Parmenides. But for method, just being a way or a path is not sufficient. It is necessary that the path be "among and through" the forms of reality. The path must be a path which is "meta," *after*. Only then will we have that which constitutes the method. Method is a problem because it is not univocally determined. And not being so is precisely why there is a meta, i.e., a forging of a way. What is this method qua intellective? That is the essential question. The matter is not resolved just by saying that method is a way of access. It is necessary to clarify the intellective character of the method itself. For this let us recall, once more, that it is a forging of a way, that is how

[8] Ibid., p. 104.

> intelligence opens in order to go from a real field thing to its worldly ground. The path is traced between two points: the real field thing and its worldly ground. Clearly one is dealing with the real thing and with its real ground, real but intellectively known, actualized, in intellection. Therefore the method is the way of access from one actualization of the real to another.[9]

Method here is not a deliberately chosen path to look into relationships between variables like say in science, but rather the inherent manner in which forms of reality collapse and proceed from one actualization to another. Let us take an example: say I am teaching a subject that students are not interested to learn. Method here is an inherent grounding of this realization that leads to the production of a fact. This constitutes a single reality field, a single gestalt that, post actualization, leads onto other gestalten. Without the grounding, the whole thing remains as an unrealized field of potentialities. And although there is no link between one objectification and another, memory carries it forward as imprint. Thus our aggregates successively move among and through the forms of reality. This movement is the method, for it seeks the ground of the reality for its actualization. Besides, all method is reciprocal and not unilateral. It is not as though some passive ground is awaiting the actualization. The ground is mysteriously emergent. The vibrating field comes in contact with the ground in which it is actualized rather like a current of electricity that remains as potential difference till it contacts the "ground," in this case, the negative terminal. "As we said, knowledge is intellection seeking itself. And what is sought is a new intellective actualization of the same real field thing. It is quite possible that the content of the ground may be something which in some way is numerically distinct from the field thing; but it is always just intellectively known as a ground of the field thing. Therefore we are dealing, strictly speaking, with a new actualization of the field thing; it is actualized not as in a field but as in the world. That it is actualized as worldly is not the same as that it is actualized as being here-and-now in the world. This last would be 'being' in the traditional sense. Here we are dealing just with reality qua respective in that respectivity which constitutes the world. And since all actualization is so of reality, it follows that ultimately what is done is to intellectively know the real more profoundly or more in-depth. That is, method is a way into reality. The moment of reality is decisive. To be sure, we are dealing with actualized

[9] Ibid., p. 106.

reality, but actualized as reality. Method is a forging of a way into reality itself towards a more profound reality. Here, 'intellection' is taken in its most radical sense, its primary sense, as the mere actualization of the real. Therefore, we are not dealing with any special actualization, as for example that of judgement, but of mere actualization regardless of its mode. Mere actualization does not exclude any special actualization, but neither can it be identified with any. Method is the way from an actualization of the real (the field actualization) to another actualization of it, actualization in the world; and it formally consists in going from one to the other by actualizing the real from its first actualization towards the second. And this process is inquiring intellection qua intellection; it is a going by intellective knowing."[10] Thus, method does not conclude in a single actualization of a field. I make an application somewhere for something and that application is not actualized. That is one actualization of the field. But then, say, that actualization leads me to seek an alternative understanding of my situation and maybe to another systemic action. So a new field arises followed by a new actualization. Method is a way we go from one actualization to the next in indefinite succession. The world is cluttered with actualized fields and realizations of fields that make their appearance as objects and phenomena, but the quest of being and becoming is to go beyond the object with an endless seeking of a deeper level of the real since all actualizations are partial. This movement is intrinsic to intelligence and not the product of any conscious volition. There exists no complete understanding of anything in reality, only an angle that comes to be in contact with the ground. And the will-to-knowledge at the heart of intellection drives the process from one actualization to the next.

> Anticipating an idea which I shall expound forthwith, I will say that knowledge starts from an actualization of the real in primordial sentient apprehension, and terminates in an actualization in a physical trial or test, i.e., a sentient trial or test of reality. The road which runs from the first to the second is just that of inquiring reason, and qua road, it is method. Method, I repeat, is an inquiring actualization of reality. Despite the inconvenience, it was essential to repeat this because the idea of method lends itself to serious confusion. Generally one understands by 'method' the path which leads from one truth to another, understanding by 'truth' a true judgement; therefore the method would be a reasoning process which goes from one true judgement to another. But to me this is untenable for three reasons. a)

[10] Ibid., p. 108.

> In the first place, method is not the way from one truth to another but from an intellectively known, actualized reality to another actualization of it. Method is not the way of truth, but the way of reality. To be sure, we are dealing with actualized reality; but it is always reality. Therefore method as path is a path not in the truth of knowledge, but in reality. In the second place, the intellection which comes into play here is not a judgement.[11]

Method is not the way of truth but a way of reality. This is an extremely significant statement. In other words, method does not consist in a series of logical steps that takes me intellectively from A to B. Rather, method is directly constructive of reality. Method is the way I am creating objects in consciousness, that is, producing reality, and moving between my productions along with myself as a co-production. Method is ontological process and progress. Hence, method is not knowledge but reality. Sentient intelligence partakes of this reality method, which is entirely different from data processing and symbolic manipulation. Here we have the case of living emergence that is multidimensional—it is simultaneously metaphysics, epistemology, and phenomenology. Those divisions are post facto expediencies and not some actual distinctions. The only reality is the living emergence from moment to moment that has all dimensions contained in it including the observer and the observed. "To be sure, actualized reality is a truth. But it is not the truth of a judgement. The intellection in which method consists is the intellection of the real as real truth, not as logical truth. In method there are judgements, clearly; but it is not judgement but real truth which determines the methodic character of intellection. In the third place, the way, the method itself, does not consist in being a reasoning process. It is not the access of a true judgement to another true judgement, because what is sought is not another judgement but another actualization. The identification of method with reasoning—which has run throughout the last centuries in all works on logic—is in my view untenable. People have fallen into this trap on account of what at various times in this study I have called the 'logification of intellection'. But it is impossible. To be sure, method is a way, and moreover is a way which must be followed; it is something to be pondered or reflected upon. But it is so in the etymological sense; it is a 'pondering' and not a logical 'discourse'. Logical discourse, the discourse of reasoning, is but a type of 'pondering'. Moreover, reasoning as such is not method. Reason has its

[11] Ibid., p. 110.

own laws, just as does the structure of judgement. But these structural laws are not method. Method, to be sure, must conform with the structural laws of logical intellection. But this conformity neither is nor can be a method which leads to knowledge, i.e., to a new actualization of the real."[12]

The truth of method is not the truth of logic or of reasoning. The truth of method spoken of here is of an originary kind which is the *truth of becoming*. We spoke of this in the example of gravity. Gravity appears as a phenomenon in the logic of intellection or logic of reasoning. In other words, a mistaken ontology enters the field through logification as already discussed. Reason is based on a split between the observer and the observed. This split is not an actuality; it is not an essential part of reality. The observer is not outside the becoming of reality, and when we place ourselves above and beyond the reality producing function, we introduce serious distortions and even allow "forces" that do not exist. Artificial or machine intelligence is a derived product that is based on a split in the reality function. Although we use the word intelligence, there is nothing intelligent in the processing of data, any more than there is in water coursing down a hill. The water may occasionally change its course due to certain build-ups, just as there might occur minor surprises in the processing of large data. But in either case there is no reflexive intellection involved.

> To intellectively know what a real thing is in reality is something which cannot be done except by intellectively knowing the real thing "from" other things of the field. But the field "from" is not identical to what I have here called 'system of reference'. In both cases one deals with a "toward", to be sure. And herein consists the similarity of the two "froms". But their respective characters are radically different. In field intellection the "toward" is a "toward" between the things of the field, and therefore we intellectively know what one of those real things is in reality from or with respect to others in the field. In field intellection one intellectively knows what something "is in reality"; therefore it is ultimately an intellection of verification or substantiation. The "from" is a chain of substantiations of what the real thing "could be". And if there is construction, it is always a construction of what would be substantiatable. On the other hand, in rational intellection one does not intellectively know what something "is in reality", but that "by which something is really in reality itself, in the world". Thus the things from which one intellectively knows this "by" are not a chain of

[12] Ibid., p. 112.

> substantiatable "could be's" but just a system of reference from which one goes to what "could be". The double meaning of the "toward" thus establishes a double mode of intellection: the intellection of what something is in field reality and the intellection of that by which something is real in the world, of what something is in universal reality itself. The first we intellectively know "from" a chain of substantiatable things; the second "from a mere system of reference". What is this system of reference? And what is its character?[13]

Conscious intellection is in part the search for the meaning of a thing, that is, its phenomenological significance as distinct from other things—the difference that makes a difference. It is the attempt to link the "to" and "from" of a thing to other "to's" and "from's." That is one kind of knowing. The other kind of knowing is the nature of the thing itself, or a sense of essence. These two kinds of knowing or intellection distinguish living intelligence from machinic ones. Sentient intelligence moves at multiple levels at once—at the reflexive level (who is this), at the intellective level (how is this), and at the essential level (what is this). "We saw that rational intellection is based upon what was previously intellectively known, and this support is just the canonic principle of intellection. Now, this canonic principle is what constitutes the system of reference. Naturally, this canonic principle is not, by itself, univocally determined. But it always has to have something, and something determined by the field. And this is now the essential point. The principle can be and is quite varied; that we shall see forthwith. But its being a principle has a precise formal character, that of being determined in accordance with the field. Therefore it is ultimately the field itself, in its field totality, that constitutes the system of reference for intellection of the world. Now, the field is a principle by virtue of its moment of reality. The field reality is the system of reference for worldly reality insofar as that field reality is reality. And this is obvious, because field and world are not two strata numerically independent—the field, as I said, is the sensed world. Now the field, what is sensed of the world, is the system of reference for the active intellection of the world. Therefore all the 'naivete' of reason always reduces to the same thing: to thinking that the world is formally identical to what is sensed of it, to the field. The field would then be the formal structure of the world. And it is

[13] Ibid., p. 116.

on this that naivete depends."[14] Is the world identical to what we sense of it? Or, rather, is the world-potentiality exhausted by what comes before the senses? Even Kant did not believe such to be the case, which is why he kept it open by speaking of the *ding-an-sich*. It takes a special kind of naivete to believe that the cosmos is qualitatively exhausted by our apprehension of it, and not only because our own appearance within it is just that, an appearance among infinitely many, but also because it is a flash in the pan, so to speak, gone before we even begin to minimally understand ourselves. What further strengthens the belief that such identity is nothing other than naivete is the fact that different cultures and even different individual consciousnesses have registered uniquely different perceptions that are at great variance from the threshold consciousness. Now, we can speak about the naivete of reason, which is the principal tool of consciousness for formalizing our relations with the field, only because of our relation to the openness that allows us to recede and reflect on the result of our objectification.

> The field is not by itself the structure of the world, but merely a system of reference. And it is so because the field is real. What happens is that it is only real in the field sense. And it is on account of its moment of reality that this field reality constitutes a principle of rational intellection. This field, as a system of reference, then has a moment upon which I wish to again insist. We are not dealing, in fact, with the field real giving us just an "idea" of what reality is. It does give us that, to be sure; but that is secondary (because it is derivative) for our problem. Nor are we dealing only with a "concept" of reality, because the field as a system of reference is not formally a concept of reality; rather it is the field "reality" itself in its own physical nature of reality. It is the physical reality of the field which, qua physical, constitutes the system of reference for the intellection of that same reality, intellectively known in the worldly sense. That intellection is therefore an activity which intellectively moves in reality itself. Granting this, what is the character of this system of reference? To be sure, it does not have representative character. It certainly involves a system of representations, because field things are already "present" and it is based upon them that we seek to present the ground. In this respect, and only in this one, they are a "representation" of this ground. But its formal function qua system of reference is not representative, because these representations do not present the ground by being representation;

[14] Ibid., p. 144.

rather, they present it only "by" grounding the sensed thing, even if to do so they destroy all the content of the representation.[15]

All philosophical systems are partial, but especially so if a philosophy maintains the observer in a transcendent position. For, in the last analysis, our system of reference has to be ourselves, collectively as a species, and nothing else. In other words, all synthesis depends on the synthesizer. So, the field must resonate and awaken something within the aggregate that we call the observer without which there is no possibility of intelligible synthesis. Without cultural familiarity, consciousness might make out the silhouette of a chair without realizing it is meant to be sat upon. This is where a system of reference comes in, and this is also the essential difference between machinic intelligence, which has no experience of sitting, leave alone sitting on a chair, and organic intelligence which has a cultural apperception of the functional use of a chair beyond its digitized coordinates. It can, even in extreme circumstances, dis-identify the chair *qua* chair and use it as a weapon to defend itself. This instant re-characterization and re-categorization is impossible without a biological reference system to which the organic intelligence refers as a matter of instinct which is not a function of time. At the street level, we call it presence of mind, but presence of mind is not a calculation nor is it dependent on algorithms, but on the groundedness of the biological being. In other words, it is not a function of time, whereas all computing including quantum computing, howsoever fast, are time-based. Another way of putting it is to say that the system of reference of which we have spoken earlier is time independent.

The representation thus has a double function: representative and directional. Only this latter makes it a system of representation. The system of reference supplies representations, but the reference itself is not in the nature of a representative. This directional function has a very precise nature. It is what I previously called 'grounding function'. The grounding function, the function of the "by", has directional character, and moreover has nothing but directional character. The representations in fact can lead to a "by" which revokes the representation or even leaves all possible representative content in suspense. Knowing is never representing. What is this directionality? And what is its cognitive status? a) Rational intellection is, as we saw, an activity, activated by the real, but nonetheless activity. Therefore the "toward" of rational intellection is an active "toward", which actively goes

[15] Ibid., p. 146.

> toward the in-depth. The system of reference consists only in the tracing out of the concrete direction of the "toward" of activity. Before I called what has been previously intellectively known 'support'; now we see that support consists in being directional reference. Directionality is concreteness of the worldly "toward" of activity. And this is essential. Knowledge is, above all, precision and exactitude, but it is a directional line. We are not dealing formally with precision and exactitude along the lines of concepts and expressions. It is quite possible that with concepts and expressions which are not univocally realized representatively, we still mark out a very precise direction. In such a case, those concepts and expressions are only partial indications of the in-depth reality, but according to a direction which is very precise in itself. That happens, for example, in quantum physics. The concepts of particle and wave are but partial representations of some aspect of the in-depth real. Their function lies in the fact that this partiality is inscribed in a precise direction which goes beyond it. Not just "complementarity", as Bohr thought, it is "superseding". The same could be said of other types of knowledge, for example the knowledge of personal realities and of living realities in general.[16]

While knowledge may ultimately reside in representation, the act of knowing is not representation. This is what sets organic knowing apart from all systems of cognitive construction, digital or not. Knowing is an active towardness which is a precise search for an inner resonance. Knowing consists of a directional reference to an a priori inner organicity which vibrates to its promptings. A good example is the findings of quantum mechanics that defy representation. In attempting to translate the findings of quantum theory into the language of everyday reality, there is a struggle to represent the wave-particle duality since nothing in ordinary experience corresponds to a dual ontological reality—such as a cat being only a probability distribution of cattiness, or being both a cat and a not-cat. The fact is that what quantum theory has found is that reality at a certain level can only have partial representation (such as wave or particle), that is, a part representation of some in-depth reality that itself cannot be represented. The actuality is more than Bohr's idea of complementarity as Zubiri states: Organic knowing *supersedes* complementarity. How then shall we speak of it?

[16] Ibid., p. 156.

> The concepts and expressions of which we make use are but aspects within a direction which is very precisely determined not just toward what we seek to intellectively know, but includes the direction of what we already intellectively know. Whence the cognitive state, so to speak, of rational intellection. Knowledge is not a system of concepts, propositions, and expressions. That would be an absurd type of conceptualism, or rather logicism, which is ultimately just formal. Moreover it would be field intellection but not knowledge. Knowledge is not just what we know and what we say, but also, and in the first place, what we want to say. Language itself is not, for the effects of intellection, something merely representative. And I am not referring to the fact that language has another dimension than that by which it is the expression of what is intellectively known. This is obvious, and a triviality. What I am now saying is that precisely as expression of rational intellection, and within this intellection, language has, besides a possible representative function, a function which differs from the merely representative. Therefore the cognitive status of the system of reference is not to serve as an explicit intellection, but something different. Anticipating some ideas that will be expounded below, I will say that in rational intellection and its expression, we are not trying to make explicit the realization of representations, but to experience a direction, to know if the direction taken is or is not of suitable precision.[17]

Organic knowing is not equivalent to formal knowledge with its concepts and expressions, which are but reconstructions and idealizations of past occurrences. Live knowing includes the inward directionality of intellection from the infinitude that surrounds us. Organocentric being is always already implicated with intellection or a directionality that is a movement rather than a terminus. As we have mentioned earlier, our desire to understand gravity is frustrated when we try to seek out some "force" as explanation. But gravity as experience becomes much clearer when we see it as a directionality—the direction of collapse of the matter-wave function. The larger mass, often seen as "attracting" smaller masses, is obviously a perceptual error. Neither the larger mass nor the smaller mass is termini in and of themselves. They are both the result of collapse-in-phase of wave densities. It is not Newton's "action-at-a-distance" but proximal and mutual collapse of the wave function that produces the experience of gravity at the surface level. We see that once the direction of intellection is in line with the reality function, there is a correct inner

[17] Ibid., p. 157.

experience, which is not a mental representation but some kind of a corporeal energetics. This also illustrates the ultimate identity between the observer and the observed—the fact that an observation perch is no different than any other. Our mental image of ourselves is nothing other than a fiction, a synthetic picture based on specific coagulation of perceptual habits. Change those habits, and we will begin to experience ourselves differently.

> What the system of reference determines is not a making [of] something explicit, but an experience. If that were not true, knowledge would never have its most valued characteristic: to be a discoverer, a creator. Hence the error which, as I see it, most radically vitiates logical positivism. In the first place, knowledge, i.e., rational intellection, is not a system of logically determined propositions. Positivism is only a conceptualization—and an incomplete one—of field intellection, but it is blind to worldly intellection, whose essential structural character is directionality. Knowledge is an intellection directed to the world from a system of reference. The formal structure of knowledge does not reduce to the formal structure of the logoi, but involves the essential moment of a directional reference. Statements with univocal meaning are not enough. Let us leave aside, for now, what logical positivism understands by 'verifiable'. In the second place, this direction is the direction of a progression. Inquiry pertains to the essence of knowledge. We are not dealing with a progression toward knowledge but with the fact that knowledge itself is intellective progression; the progression is just its own mode of intellection.[18]

Take the case of dark electrons—electrons that supposedly do not absorb photons and are therefore not detectable. If we stop with the electron, dark or not, then we remain within the existing level of description, only expanding its scope. In other words, we apply yet another layer of mystification over the previous layers of mystifications—the electron, after all, is a polite fiction selected from among several possible models. We cannot intellectively know anything about a phenomenon by calling it an electron or by giving it any other name. The mental or verbal representation is always an inadequate, and even misleading, source of knowledge. It is misleading because we begin to believe in the actuality of the representation. But the description is not the described. Sentient intelligence on the other hand bypasses the representation in an organocentric direction since

[18] Ibid., p. 169.

it already possesses a vast and dynamic intelligence that maintains its living viability. In other words, we can learn to "see" things in the core of our corporeal being without necessarily making mental representations. In this view, the old notion of intellection as a purely mental phenomenon is replaced by a more holistic view. At the core of intellection is something that may be called potency or "fertility." This fertility or fecundity is the innate power and desire to seek new direction that is the essence of the living or the sentient.[19] Machines or machinic capabilities do not include potency or fertility since they are merely logical and not bio-logical. In the bio-logical we include complex *qualities* such as motivation, ethics, integrity, altruism, empathy, humor, fear, and desire that form the obverse or complementary side of the logical without which the distinctions made in consciousness are impossible because there is an absence of what may be called a towardness or phenomenological intentionality.

> Positivism limits itself to the logical statements of this intellection. But those statements are only its logical expression; they do not constitute the formal structure of the knowledge which is intellective progression. In the third place, this progression is creative. Logical positivism is blind to this third, creative dimension of knowledge, because creating is not stating new propositions but discovering new directions of intellective progression. It is for this reason that the cognitive status of rational intellection is not to be a "univocal" manifestation but a "fertile" direction toward the worldly real. This fertility is not a consequence of rational intellection but a formally structural moment of it. To be sure, I believe that today philosophy, perhaps more than ever, must have conceptual precision and formal rigor. Modern philosophy is in this regard the source of a great deal of confusion which gives rise to erroneous interpretations. I have strongly emphasized this: the reconquest of exactitude and precision in concepts and expressions is necessary. But this does not in any sense mean that such analysis, which is the function of logic, is the structure of knowledge, because the world does not have a logical structure but rather a real respectivity. And only because of this is knowledge what it is: the progression toward the system of reality. The inquiring activity of rational thinking makes its second essential step within this system or reality.

Our intellectual tradition, especially in the sciences, is stuck in the attitude of positivism till this day. Let me illustrate this by citing a single

[19] The word fertile comes from OF *ferre* and ultimately PIE/Skt *urvara* (*uru* "much" and *r* "to go"). We may say that one possible meaning could be the power to go beyond.

instance of personal experience as a teacher in a primarily science and technology institute. Proposed courses here, even when related to general humanities, acquire legitimacy merely by appending AI—I am witness to bizarre course titles such as "Artificial Intelligence and International Relations," and suchlike. The attempt to gain legitimacy by technologizing everything is a blind urge to get away from complex uncertainties of existence. And the response to it comes from the residual impulse within the positivist-empiricist attitude of world-as-data, together with the promise of a managed society. The latter, since it is the principal attitude in modern technology-dominated societies, finds nothing particularly problematic in equating the experience of reality with the formalizations of it. This is the essential step in maintaining the world-as-data paradigm, for data requires systematic treatment and this systematization in turn rests on the belief that the understanding of the world is exhausted by the formal statements about it. We become blind to the fact that there are many other ways and means of constructing reality. In actuality, the world is nothing but an infinite variety of raw materials (frequencies and amplitudes) and modes of organizing them (phased coherencies), with the organizing principles themselves being among the organized. In other words, intellection, which is a mode of self-constitution that reciprocally organizes both the observer and the observed, is fundamentally a creative process, and not a subset of the superset of the logically expressed.

Logical positivism makes the fundamental error of mistaking mental representations and their logical expressions for constitutive freedom. It is in this constitutive freedom that intellective progression has meaning. Looking out over the car park and all the tall buildings in sight and the vapor trail of aircraft overhead, one might be overwhelmed with the need for something else altogether besides and beyond civilizational accumulation. Likewise, in the search for adequate explanation of something, one might be overcome by the need for a new schema or model. Again, thinking of one's damaged life one might be driven to seek an alternative existence shedding the cocoon of the previous trappings. All of these and more are instantiations of the seeking of constitutive potentiality within any situation. In each of these cases, an outcome may be ultimately expressed and documented as part of the formal process of expression, but intellective progression or the creative dimension of knowledge cannot be captured and would not be part of that expression. In other words, the surplus potential always escapes, and what is left are the historical remains of a process. Therefore, Zubiri says that creation is not the stating of new propositions but "discovering new directions of intellective progression." The cognitive force of sentient intelligence lies not within formalized expressions (which are but the conceptualized history of previous experience), but in a fertile directionality toward fresh compositions and engagements with the potentiality of the world. No doubt, we must have certitude in the concepts and expression we use, but this does not imply that the underlying world about which these concepts and expressions speak is somehow akin to them. In other words, we must not make the grave mistake of thinking that the world is patterned or structured after the manner in which we structure our logical representations of it, whether, mathematical, physical, biological, or something else. The world is not necessarily analogous to how we think about the world; it is instead an unimaginable potentiality with infinite possible variations continually emergent from it. That is why Zubiri says that the world does not have a logical structure but rather a real respectivity. Logic is only a minor development within a specific path of biological evolution or respectivity of the species. It cannot hope to reveal the world as it is, but only structure and accommodate the infinite potentiality and materiality that lends itself as a towardness, or an intentionality toward composite objectification. "Since antiquity the idea that natural science rests importantly on experience has been non-controversial. The only real questions about the sources of scientific knowledge are: Are there parts of science that do not rest on experience or rest also on something other than experience? If so what account can we give of those parts? And to the extent that science does rest on experience how can we know that it does? There is another question about science related to these, though not strictly about the sources of science, and that is: Why, in making claims about the world, should we be scientific as opposed to, say, mystical? The difficulty is that any scientific answer to this last question would reasonably be thought to beg the very question it purports to address."[20] To say that natural science rests on experience is somewhat tautological. It isn't as though natural science was ruminating on an unfiltered, pristine nature. Our observation is always already delimited by the selections made by our cognitive attitude—what we are able to

[20] Richard Creath, "Logical Empiricism", *The Stanford Encyclopedia of Philosophy* (Winter 2023 Edition), Edward N. Zalta & Uri Nodelman (eds.), URL = <https://plato.stanford.edu/archives/win2023/entries/logical-empiricism/>.

take into account, and what we are not.[21] Therefore, from what we have discussed so far, natural science itself is the accumulated objectification of reality by means of methodical activity—the so-called scientific method. Among many possibilities, it selects an explanation for observed phenomena through logical means and affirms or rejects it through experimentation. But now, if we ask the reflexive question as to what undergirds the scientific method itself, then we are in trouble. After a point, is it then "turtles all the way down" as the saying goes? In other words, at some point do we have to accept the equating of reality with our constructs?

> What is the formal terminus of this methodical activity? We have already seen the answer: it is what a field thing "could be" in the world. The formal terminus of cognitive activity is the ground of the real as possibility. For the effects of rational intellection, the ambit of grounding, the world, is in the first place the ambit of the possibilities of the ground. The world is certainly reality, the respectivity itself of the real as real. But this reality, for the effects of knowledge, is only the ambit of intellection of the ground. And as intellection is actualization, it follows that the actuality of the world in intellection is actualization of all the possibilities of the ground. But this requires further clarification. Consider the matter of possibilities. They are real possibilities, i.e., possibilities which are comprised as such in the intellection n of the real world (not a redundancy). What are these real possibilities? Above all, they are possibilities in the sense that they are that which the real perhaps "could be" in the worldly sense. That we have already seen. We are not dealing with a mere "might be" but with a "could be", i.e., with a positive mode of the making possible of the real. The real is not just what it is, but is something modally real constituted from its own ground, based on its own, intrinsic, and formally real possibilities. As possibilities, they are in themselves something unreal; but the unreal, realized as a ground of reality, is the very possibility of the real, what intrinsically and formally is making it possible. The real is something essentially possibilitated. It is not that possibility is prior to reality, but that the mode of reality of the worldly is to be possibilitated as real; possibility is only a mode of reality. Why? Because of its own insertion into the world. In this sense, possibility is not prior to the real, but a modal moment of its worldly respectivity. It is because of this that I speak of possibilitation rather than possibility. But this possibilitation also has another essential aspect. Every intellective actualization is so of reality, but at the same time is intellective. Now, with respect to a rational intellection,

[21] For instance, science has never been comfortable with mystical perception, or with intuitive methods.

> the intellection itself is activity. Hence it follows that the possibility of the "could be" is at one and the same time the possibility of the "could be" of the real thing and the "could be" of the intellection. This intellection is an inquiring activity. Therefore, in this second aspect, the possibilities take on the character of what we call the 'possibilities of my activity', something completely different from my potencies and faculties. The system of reference, I said, is the concrete outline of the toward.[22]

The important points raised above in terms of our discussion are as follows: The formal end of intelligent cognitive activity including scientific inquiry leads to pointing toward the ground of potentialities, or what is called the field. The field object is not the actual object of experience, but the liquid probabilities of the ground. Sentient intellection is actualization "within the ambit of intellection," but this does not imply that these are somehow pre-existing as some kind of thing-in-waiting. That is why it is stated that possibility is only a mode of reality reciprocally activated when sentient seeking enters the picture. Only when sentient intelligence enters the picture the potentialities of the real are manifested as the field. It is therefore clear that no artificial simulation can make this field appear, for the artificial simulation is already a dead or objectified product. This alone destroys any attempt at drawing a parallel between organic or sentient intelligence and artificial copies; the latter cannot elicit the field which is the prerogative of the bio-organic brought about in a field of mutuality through the natural evolution of intellection. It cannot be simulated. Take the case of a human AI generator or programmer. In generating a program, s/he is excluding an infinity of possibilities of directing her/his living energy-time and producing a program. The generated program cannot access those potentialities, but can only work within what is already matured in the world of the real. In other words, the AI program will be at best a small subset of what is already realized in the field of the real. That is to say, it can only get to the *techne* and not to the *poiesis* of the reality field.

> Only a sentient intelligence knows by sketch; the sketch is only for knowledge. Conversely, a sentient intelligence can only know by sketching. In our problem, sketching is an act which is purely and formally intellective, and this activity is a mode of intellection; it is intellection activated by the real itself. Consequently, we are not here dealing with a human activity "applied"

[22] Zubiri, op. cit., p. 219.

to intellection, or anything like it. Activity is intellection activated by the real, and the sketch, as an act of this activity, is something formally intellective—indeed, it is the very intellection of the possible ground. The ground is only knowable to us by sketching, because the sketch is the concrete form of illumination of possibilities (real ones and of intellection). An activity that sketches is the only place where one can actualize reality as a possibility both real and of intellection. Sketching is a form of intellective knowing. How does one sketch the actuality of the real in its possibility? The possibilities are not sketched other than by confronting the field real in intellective activity, i.e., intellectively knowing the field as real worldly object. The confronting is what on the one hand converts the real into something that can be grounded, i.e., it is what constitutes the real upon the base of its possibility.[23]

Let me illustrate the idea of the "sketch" with an example. There is a picture of a set of eyes, with one fully open and the other almost shut. Let us call this a "sketch" and proceed to ask for an analysis of what is going on here. There are a number of possibilities, including the case that it is a wink, or that it is the parody of a wink, or that there is dust in the eye, or that it is a nervous twitch, or even a completely novel explanation. The interpretation will depend on the surrounding actualizations or what we call the context. With a minimum of information, the sentient intelligence can come up with an intellective action based on the context and the probabilities organically associated with it. Most of the intellective actions of organic intelligence are based on sketches; it is astoundingly economical, and allows the active intelligence even to review the conclusion any number of times balancing out the probabilities and even changing its mind. All of this the organic intelligence does, sometimes without even being aware of it. It does so not by means of processing but in empathetic confrontation with the field that contains the "plasma" of reality. And this includes changing tracks abruptly and radically and reconfiguring in the intellective direction, and even coming up with new composites that are post-civilizational.

Possibility thus illuminated has its own content. This content qua possibility is always something constructed; it is construction. (I am not speaking of construction in the sense of, say, group theory). The sketch of possibilities is always just a constructed sketch. No intellective possibility as such is purely and simply given. It may be received if entrusted to us; that is the problem

[23] Ibid., p. 223.

> of history as transmission. But that is another question. What is here important to us is that what is entrusted is a construction. It could likewise be that the construction consists only in accepting as possibility the real which is encountered. But even in this case, clearly what is encountered is converted into a possibility, i.e., is something constructed; immediate construction if one wishes, but still construction. In this construction, each of its moments is a possibility. Therefore the construction is properly construction of a system of possibilities. The system of reference is for the construction of a system of possibilities. Each possibility is only making possible within a system together with the rest. We already saw this when dealing with possibility as formal terminus of rational intellection. The possibilities are not added together but rather "co-possibilitate". And this "co-" is the system. Therefore every alteration of a possibility implies in principle, if not the alteration, then the reconsideration of all the rest. The crisis of a possibility puts the entire system in crisis.[24]

There are multiple ways of encountering the content of situations, objects, and relationships. The commonplace one is to receive it as it has been handed down in terms of its immediate constituted structure—we receive it in terms of a certain givenness or a historical transmission. A very different way to see what is encountered is in terms of its constitutive possibilities, or what might be called its plasmic content, and look for the intellective directions it suggests. Here we convert the encountered in terms of its directional possibilities and potentialities, deconstructing it into a large number of constituent moments. None of these constituent moments are given by themselves, but come out of the mode of reckoning. That is to say, no intellective possibility is received as a given, but must be actively converted into a possibility through intellection. Let us take an example to see how it branches out into a system of possibilities. Let us consider the case of a national constitution. The people can receive it as a historical transmission that constitutes the fundamental and directive principles of state policy. But in the possibilities view, the document may be deconstructed along its lines of becoming to reveal a set of directional dynamics. We can, for instance, seek in it the ideal of the constituent citizen built into the structure that the constitution makers assumed. Again, we can seek in it the psycho-social and ideological make-up of the makers and their assumptions about social relations. We can seek in it the differences in thought and practice when it comes to the delivery of justice. We

[24] Ibid., p. 235.

can even isolate the contradictions and conflicts inherent in the historical document. And so on and on. The deconstruction releases a system of possibilities and courses of action for fresh becomings within and beyond it.

> This system of possibilities is not univocally determined. Therefore its constitution is a free construction. All of its intrinsic limitations follow from this, limitations with respect to its capacity to lead to the sought-after ground. That capacity is "fecundity". The system of possibilities, by virtue of being freely constructed, is of limited fecundity. But it has still another limitation: it is a system selected from among others. In virtue of this, the system is of limited "amplitude". When the ground for a system of possibilities is known, this knowledge is limited in fecundity and amplitude. Hence its constitutive openness. All knowledge, by virtue of being an intellection with a system of possibilities freely constructed from a system of reference, is an open knowledge, not just in fact and because of human, social, and historical limitations. Rather, it is open qua knowledge through intrinsic necessity, to wit, by being intellection as sketch. And this is a moment which is formally constitutive of rational intellection as such. The second step of the method is the sketch of this system of possibilities from a system selected as the reference. But the method as a way seeks to lead to an end, viz. intellection of the ground of the real. This is the third step of method, the final step. The first is the establishment of a system of reference; the second is the sketching of possibilities; and the third is the intellection of the possibilitating ground of the real.[25]

The ontology of becoming is bounded by many degrees of freedom (variables) beyond simply the will-to-become. The total capacity is the potential or fecundity of the system of possibilities. The possible constructions within this system are free by virtue of not being determined one-sidedly by any particular will, and at the same time being limited by the degree of fertility (amplitude) of the system of references. Being free and limited at the same time makes organic intellection constitutively open. This openness is characteristic of the autopoiesis of the sentient, as contrasted with the capabilities of the non-organic, which is univocal being determined by the algorithm and not by any system of possibilities or fertility beyond it. The marvel of organic intellection can be illustrated by the following example. Consider the case of a crash survivor who experiences financial, physical, and emotional shock due to an accident. On

[25] Ibid., p. 236.

recovery, the individual may go back to her/his routine life, or may realize that the life prior to the accident is no longer interesting or worth living. Now, the individual is faced with a whole array of existential possibilities. But, first, these choices are not univocally determined, since they are framed by other conditions. This establishes the system of references. Second, within this system of references lie the possibilities or fecundities that appear as a sketch in the intellective search. Finally, there is the intellective moment of actualizing a possibility. The intricate nature of this organic intellection cannot be mimicked by a non-organic system simply because, first, non-organic systems do not come out of a non-finite or indeterminable ground of co-possibilities but from a specific set of algorithmic possibilities. Second, the system of references from which the non-organic picks a pattern (sketch) from large data sets is closed since the database is pre-specified and not a co-possibility. Finally, the process of making a definite choice is not linked to any future possibility, unlike in the organic in which the intellective moment is linked to future expectations, and therefore open.

> How does one intellectively know the possibilitating ground of the real as worldly reality? When one intellectively knows this ground, the knowledge has reached its terminus. This is the problem of the access to what one seeks to know. Method is nothing if it does not lead to a real and effective access. Now, with the proviso that I shall explain myself further below, let me say that access is, formally, experience. Knowing begins with a system of reference from which one sketches a system of possibilities which permit one to experience what a thing is as worldly reality. To clarify this we need to conceptualize what experience is, what one finds in experience (i.e., the experienced), and what is the mode of finding it. That is, we seek the concept of experience, the object of experience, and mode of experience. A) What is experience? Experience is not a univocal concept. When we speak of experience, generally we think in terms of what is called 'sensible experience'. And this is extremely ambiguous, because the expression has different meanings, all completely acceptable for a language, but not identical in conceptualization either to "sensible" or to "experience", as we shall see. What do we understand by 'sensible'? And above all, what do we understand by 'experience'? A first meaning for 'experience', and one which is very general, is perception, aísthesis, i.e., sensing, and hence the sensed qualities. In this sense experience is opposed to what would be intellective apprehension. The so-called 'sensualism' thus philosophically understands that experience is perception (external or internal, it matters little). To have an experience of

> something would be to perceive it. But this is absolutely unacceptable. If I may be permitted the expression, to experience is not to sense. And this is true in a very radical sense. In the first place, sensing does not only sense qualities but also that these qualities are real. We have not only an impression of green (strictly speaking it is impossible to only have the impression of green), but also the impression of green as real. Sensualism has seriously gone astray with respect to this matter. What is sensed in experience is not only a quality but also its formality of reality. Therefore human sensing is intellective, since apprehending something as real is the formally constitutive part of intellection.[26]

Consider someone watching a horror film. If the organic consciousness believed that what was going on was congruent with the actuality, then s/he may show signs of deep distress or even be traumatized. What protects the viewing consciousness from becoming excessively disturbed is the simultaneous awareness that this is not for real. How does it develop this double consciousness? It is experience that allows us to know that what is being currently experienced is not the actuality but a simulation. We know it through the cues such as the screen and the surrounding reality that do not form part of the goings-on. If these cues are absent, as in a dream, there would be a confounding between the simulation or nightmare and actuality, occasionally resulting in actual distress. But in waking moments, the consciousness is pointed toward the ground of reality and therefore can leave the distressing situation at will. Here we see that there is a system of reference whose presence can clearly distinguish the film from the reality. A simulated reality within an actuality cannot fool an organic consciousness due to the fact that it has multiple levels of experiencing going on at the same time. It can weep at the suffering of an on-screen character, and simultaneously be embarrassed and feel silly for doing so. And in fact, these conflicting signals can produce a third order inner experience that is totally unexpected—a moment of surprise. We can lapse into being schizoid momentarily, and then be free of the schizoid-ness after a moment, when the ground of reality regains a unitariness. This is due to the nature of organic experience. To say it is non-linear is to say nothing. Organic consciousness is personal or individual only up to a point; it comes from an evolutionary line whose origin is not available to us, and which provides us with an evolved context for the ground of reality which is a kind

[26] Ibid., p. 233.

of participation and co-evolution. This co-evolution or participation is ultimately aesthetic, and cannot be mimicked by any closed system or machinic capacity however sophisticated. In other words, sentient intelligence is not glorified machine learning, nor is machinic cognition an abridged or incomplete form of the organic. The two belong to vastly different ontological categories, whose superficial cognitive resemblance must not be stretched beyond a point, notwithstanding all the fuss around the Turing machine.

> Moreover, in the second place, not even understanding sensing as intellective sensing is it acceptable to identify experiencing and sensing. To be sure, without sensing there is no experience; but to sense is not formally to experience. In sensing, what is sensed is something fundamentally given. Now, what is experienced is not something given but something achieved—achieved certainly by sensing, but still achieved. The sensible is just the experienciable, but is not formally experienced. The moment of achievement is essential to experience. What does this moment mean? One might think that experience consists in the experience of "one thing", and not simply of some quality. It might be that this thing is a quality, but be that as it may, it might be the terminus of an experience only insofar as that quality is considered as a thing. Now, anything real, considered as a thing, even in the most stable of cases, is something variable and fleeting. Experience would not be just sensing, but that habitude of sensing something as fixed and stable.[27]

Here is a very important moment in the argument. Sense experience concerns a givenness—there is a latent assumption that what is sensed existed prior to sensing. We rarely think of sense experience as the bringing forth of something, or something that is achieved. And this objectivity of sensing is partly due to the fact that there are others besides the sensor or experiencer who share the same experience. But experience is really a way of stabilizing what is sensed. It is a habit of stability. One senses one's partner which becomes a habitual way of responding, and therefore I say I experience my partner. But each moment of the partner is unique and different, each angle is different, each mood is different, each affection is different, and out of those differences an overriding habit of sameness is born. Hence we can say that what is experienced is in a sense achieved. This achievement is not a machinic synthesis but an organic poiesis due to

[27] Ibid.

the fact that it is not held together by data alone but by expectations. How can we claim that? Imagine a scenario in which my partner fails to appear at the place where we were supposed to meet. The machine would simply register a nil return. My reaction from previous experience would be to panic and start making calls, and when that fails maybe to start doing stupid things. The machine cannot suddenly turn illogical and do unpredictable things, or achieve stupidity; it can only carry out mechanically optimum ones. Hence we say that experience, in actuality, is a bringing forth, and not simply the sensing of the given. It might use data, but it is much more than the mechanical, high-speed synthesis of information. The ontology of its *energeia* is different from the mere electrical impulse of the machine. Consciousness is an active seeking with its nose pointed toward the "plasma" of the ground from where it brings forth the experience of reality. The machine, on the other hand, simply follows its program howsoever sophisticated, in the inexorable manner of water running its course, and does not, cannot, stop and wonder if it's all worth it. That's the difference.

> Sensing senses quality (I add, real quality), but experience might be a mode of sensing something "itself". This is the concept of experience which Aristotle crafted and which he called empeiría. Aristotle thought that the constitutive moment of experience is the mnéme, retention; thus the reiteration of perception, the retained perception, would be experience. But this is inadequate. Experience is not necessarily that which Aristotle called empeiría, because what is perceived and retained is not only the quality but, as I keep repeating, the formality of reality. Aristotle definitively separated the sensible and the intelligible, and therefore never conceptualized that intellective sensing whose formal moment I have called 'impression of reality'. Experience is not just empirical sameness. The empeiría is only a mode of experience. And the proof is the fact that we speak of people who have much or little experience of a thing or situation. The sameness in question is hence not a mere empirical retention of qualities nor of a real quality; rather, what is retained must be just a real thing intellectively known (retentively if one wishes) as real, not in each of its perceptive phases, but as real in the worldly sense. The experiential moment is not, then, empirical retentiveness, but something different. What? That is the third concept of experience. When we speak of not having experience or of having much or little experience of something, we are not referring to the diversity of perceptive acts of a thing, even if perceived as real; rather, we refer to that mode of apprehending it (including perceptively) which consists in intellectively knowing it in depth.

> The achievement which constitutes experience is an achievement of reaching this depth, not the moment of retentive sameness.[28]

Here we come upon a critical distinction in the course of our findings: Sentient intelligence does not experience everything in a uniform manner or with identical intensity. We do not merely sense things but experience them differentially at varying impressional depths. The differential depth of experience is not empirical retention or memory but perceptual quality of a different order. On the other hand, mechanical cognition or AI is essentially dependent upon data and the retention of data (memory). Even when the data simulates a 3-D environment as in laser mapping it is simply extending the physical depth dimension and not the qualitative depth of the impression. This is due to the fact that quality is not a number and so cannot be given a numerical value. And yet this quality is what determines the impressions we hold as important and those that we discard or are forgotten quickly. The architecture of a structure or a particular scene remains with us for the rest of our lives, even though, from the cognitive standpoint, or in terms of neural mapping, there may be nothing particularly distinctive about the structure or the scene. What we see here is the emergence of "significance" or meaning, both terms being ultimately difficult to define. But it is the differential intensities of impression that ultimately imbues a perceptive act with significance. Thus, when we know something deeply, it is not the breadth of knowledge that is being referred, but rather the mode of apprehending that resonates and touches a nerve within us, as it were. In the teaching-learning situation, an identical set of information coming from A may leave a lasting effect on B, but not the same effect on C. In a similar vein, X and Y may speak of the same thing but leave very different impressions on Z. In distinguishing sentient intelligence from machinic cognition it is this depth dimension or quality of apprehension that is critically important. For on this depends that which we call the creative impulse, of which we will have more to say toward the end of the present discussion.

> By reaching this depth, the thing is actualized as worldly reality. Therefore, in order to know what experience is, we must say what reaching this depth is as a mode of intellective actualization. So we are dealing with an actualization, but not as mere actualization. That would be just sentient intellection,

[28] Ibid., p. 249.

> not experience. Something more than naked reality is needed; it is the real which actualizes what "really" is. Therefore, we actualize its reality as referred to other things which open an ambit within which the thing takes on its possible respect to these other things. And in order to intellectively know what we seek to intellectively know, the indicated things are those which outline, in intellection, the characteristics of that real thing. As such, this outline is thus something unreal in itself. Now, this unreal thing has to be intellectively known as inserted in the real thing; only thus will it be the outline of it. And this insertion can have two different modalities. a) The unreal can be inserted into the real by being actualized in the real as a realization. This is the realization of the unreal in the real. Intellection then consists in intellectively knowing what the real thing is in reality. To realize is to intellectively know the reality of the "could be". It is in this realization that being a manifestation consists. It is the intellection of the real in the field sense. b) But the unreal can be inserted and actualized in the real in a different way, by testing if it is inserted. This is not manifestation, i.e., it is not mere realization, but testing. We then intellectively know by testing what the real thing is in depth. What is this testing? It is not, formally, just an assay or experiment. It is something else. In the first place, it is testing of reality. This reality is not naked reality nor a realization, but the reality of the thing as a moment of the world. Reality here is not of the field but of the world. It is not the realization of a "might be" but of a "could be". Because of this, as we shall see, such realization is testing. Testing rests upon the "beyond". It is something essentially different from a manifestation. What is in reality is manifested; what could be is tested. In the second place, this is a physical testing. We are not dealing with a thought experiment, or anything of that nature. We are dealing with a "physical" testing. It is something not thought but carried out. It is "to do" the testing. And this exercise has an essential character. It is something carried out, but the carrying out itself is a mode of intellection of the real in its worldly character.[29]

In sentient intellection as distinct from machinic cognition there are two distinct modes. The first is manifestation. When reality itself provides the impulse from some unknown ground for something to be actualized, then we have a manifestation. A cyclone or an earthquake is a manifestation. We merely experience the effects of that manifestation in a passive mode. "The unreal can be inserted into the real by being actualized in the real as a realization." Intellection here consists of knowing or identifying the manifestation of that which was up until that point a potentiality.

[29] Ibid., p. 251.

When we feel tremors, we intellectively know that there is a shifting of the ground to which we have given a name. This mode of referencing is to identify the characteristics of something whose reality is manifested from an unreality. "This is the realization of the unreal in the real." But there is also a realization in the real that is not merely a manifestation. I seek intensely for something, and the thing I pray for comes to be. This is sending out a signal of intensity into the ground of the real as a kind of testing. It rests upon the beyond, but that beyond is not manifested; what is experienced is a world-moment which is intellectively recognized. In other words, I carry out a "test" in seeking out reality as a mode of intellective becoming.

> There is another mode of experience which consists, not in making a thing show us its own nature by some provocation of ours, but in the attempt to be present, so to speak, at the vision of the real achieved based on its own interiority. To be sure, the merely material reality of an atom or molecule is not viable in this form; but it is something possible and real when dealing with living realities and above all human realities. This being present is grounded upon an installation of the one experiencing in the experiential; it is what I call compenetration. Life in general, and above all human life, is subject to the physical testing of reality, not just as an experimental fact, but as reality in compenetration. Naturally we are not dealing with some physical penetration, but of being compenetrated with what makes one experience. It is what is expressed upon saying, for example, that someone sees through the eyes of another. It is a type of perikhoresis, not of reality but of the modes of actuating, and of conducting oneself. It is a difficult operation; one always runs the risk of projecting the nature of the one experiencing upon what is experienced. But be that as it may, this is an authentic mode of rational intellection, an authentic mode of physical testing of reality. Compenetration is a rigorous mode of experience. To be sure it is not experiment; but without excluding experiment, compenetration actualizes, in a worldly way, the real in the intellection of the one experiencing. There is no better knowledge of a person than that which is achieved by being compenetrated with him. And this extends to all of the dimensions of human life. Moreover, it extends to merely animal life and up to a certain point, to vegetable life as well. When all is said and done, we describe the life of an animal by realizing with some difficulty the experience of compenetrating with it given the limits of its biological constitution. I said that this extends to all dimensions of human life. Thus, for example, leaving aside the problem

of its truth, there is, as a mode of physical testing of reality, a strict historical experience.[30]

There is a third mode of intellective experience which is a kind of intuitive co-knowing. This is "possible and real when dealing with living realities and above all human realities." In other words, living intelligences mutually can experience empathetic co-knowledge of another in a way that machinic cognition cannot. An acute and intrinsic awareness of the other: "two things are needed for perichoresis: difference and unity. For, how could any perichoresis or permeation make sense without the difference? And without the unity, it would mean that permeation or perichoresis did not happen at all; namely, permeation necessarily leads to union, to the state of unity. But what is peculiar to the permeation, what makes perichoresis a very special unity, different both from mixing and merging, is the fact that despite this unity, the difference is not lost—it still exists. In perichoresis, therefore, what is different becomes united without losing its difference. We know that the notion of unity or union is an important concept in the mystical and dogmatic theology, well grounded in a number of scriptural texts. Let us only remember the Jesus': "The Father and I are one" (John 10:30). However, the precious light which perichoresis sheds on that unity consists in that it also expresses preservation of the difference in that unity. Therefore, although the notion of perichoresis implicitly expresses both previously known concepts of inexistence and unity, it also includes an additional element not explicitly present in these notions, and that additional element consists of the preservation of difference. But this is not the only additional element. We could already see that perichoresis also implicitly expresses the idea of communication of attributes, which is a special and important effect of permeation. In addition, it could be also noted that perichoresis is both an act and the state at the same time. Namely, as we have already said, permeation is an act of entering and spreading through or within something, but it necessarily results in the state of permeation, which is the state of union. … Thus, neither the human nature turned into the divine, nor the divine turned into the human, but either of them, each retaining its own nature, became permeated with the other, and because of this deep interpenetrating union they communicate to each other their own attributes. Here we see that perichoresis at the same time stands as the ground of what is known in

[30] Ibid., p. 256.

theology as communicatio idiomatum. Therefore, without understanding the perichoresis one cannot see how is this communication of attributes possible at all without any changes in the natures."[31] The phenomenon of perichoresis demands two apparently opposed things at the same time—distinction and union. This qualitative commingling while retaining the distinctive self-natures is a remarkable possibility of sentient intelligence. It is remarkable not merely because there is no parallel for this in machinic cognition, but because it is this opening that makes the evolutionary transition to another state an ontological possibility. In *Letter to the Romans*, when Paul writes that a remainder will be saved, he is alluding to the coming of a godliness that will mix with the worthy and emancipate them. But for that one must prepare oneself, which suggests a kind of perichoresis or a co-penetration of strikingly different qualities that bring about a new or more intensely alive state. Perichoresis thus also suggests an extraordinary pedagogic moment in which the known is invaded by the unknown.

The strange interchange between the known and the unknown is seen in distinctly other domains too making intellection of living intelligence a unique process. The Incompleteness Theorem of Gödel showed that in any closed system, there are propositions that can neither be proved right nor wrong within that system, but remain as undecidables. One way to think of it is that mathematical properties are not merely logical, but are mixed up with the real in some way.

> Gödel demonstrated that what is postulated has properties which are not deducible from the postulates nor can they be logically refuted by them. The fact is, as I see it, that they are real properties of mathematical reality, and their apprehension independent of the postulates is a point in which the apprehension of reality does not coincide with logical intellection. In every mathematical method there is, then, a double moment: the moment of necessary truth of an affirmation, and the moment of apprehension of reality. One's necessarily affirming that reality is thus, is not opposed to the fact that the moment of reality is formally distinct from the logical necessity of my affirmation. To be sure, they are two moments of a single, unique act; but as moments they are different. And in them the moment of logical necessity is not primary because the postulates in turn do not consist in logical affirmations but in postulations of the content of reality. It is reality, then, which has the first and last word in all mathematical intellection. These two

[31] Stamatović, Slobodan. "The Meaning of *Perichoresis*," *Open Theology*, vol. 2, no. 1, 2016. https://doi.org/10.1515/opth-2016-0026.

> moments, the moment of truth and the moment of apprehension of reality, nonetheless have an intrinsic unity. It is what I call testing-together [comprobar] or verifying. As I see it, verification does not consist in verifying if my affirmation is verified; that does not need to be verified in mathematics. What is verified is not the truth of my affirmation but the very presence of the apprehended through a way of logical deduction. It is the testing or verifying of reality through the "together" of truth. Truth is not verified, but rather the reality in its truth; we apprehend "reality in truth". This might make it seem that the method has consisted of a reasoning process. But this is not true because all reasoning processes depend upon something prior to the reasoning itself, upon the postulation of the content of reality.[32]

We have been taught to believe that logical propositions have no materiality, but are abstract rules free of context or content. But the discovery that rules within a system are inherently limited by closure, and cannot help to decide all propositions in that system point to the fact there must be real properties mixed in it, for the perception that something is inconsistent cannot be made from within the inconsistent process itself, but must be made by a supervening process. Inconsistency is a material judgment and must be a real decision on a meta level. This means that the determination of the status of something is not identical to the interchanges within a system, but the work of a different order of intelligence. The moment of reality is formally distinct from the logical necessity of one's affirmation of it—the two moments may be perichoretically intermingled but nevertheless distinct. This is characteristic of sentient intelligence—it simultaneously works at two distinct perceptive levels, meta (presence) and infra (process), which are in constant communication with each other. "It is reality, then, which has the first and last word in all of mathematical intellection," although it is sanitized and made to seem as though propositional calculus stands outside of the reality content. Mechanical processes involve only a unitary level of processing. Thus, "Method is a path into postulated reality, an oriented path in accordance with logical rigor. But if this demonstrative rigor, by being impossible, did not lead us to apprehend the reality of A as 'being' B, we would not have mathematics. The unity of the two moments of the intellection of postulated reality is, then, what we call 'verification'. The physical testing [probación] of reality is now verification [comprobación]. Here we have the essence of what, paradoxically, but very exactly, should be called the

[32] Zubiri, op. cit., p. 253.

'experience of the mathematical'. The mathematical is the terminus of a physical testing of reality, of experience. To be sure, there are postulated realities which are not mathematical; they constitute the ambit of the reality of fiction. But I need not insist upon them because however they are seen, they have the two moments of internal coherence of the feigned, and of apprehension of its reality in fiction. They are, in this sense, the terminus of verification, in explicit form. Every postulated reality has, then, a mode of experience its own, verification."[33] Although reality and the method of verifying can only run parallel to each other and never be made into an identity, as these are qualitatively different in nature, we would not have the experience of mathematics were it not for the applied effort of trying to make one moment look like the other. So here we have a paradoxical situation, wherein the impossibility of an identity between the inherently non-identical makes the experience of a feigned identity a possibility—"the two moments of internal coherence of the feigned, and of apprehension of its reality in fiction." It is the apprehension of reality in the feigned—the experience of identity within non-identity.

Further, living intelligence when it turns toward itself appears paradoxical in trying to verify its own reality.

> But there is still another mode of experience, the mode which concerns the nature of my experiencing my own reality. It is the experience of myself. Above all, what does 'experience of myself' mean here? To be sure, we are not dealing with the mere apprehension of my reality; that happens, as we have already seen, due to sentient intellection of a general sense of corporeal existence. Nor are we dealing with a mere affirmation of what I am or am not in reality, i.e., with a mere judgement of field intellection. To say that what I really am in the field of my violent reactions, perhaps being a timid person, is not a rational intellection of what I am as worldly reality. We are dealing, then, not with a mere apprehension of my reality, nor with a judgement of what I am in reality, but with an intellection of what my reality is as a form of reality, i.e., with a rational intellection, with knowledge. This form of reality has the two moments of being a mode of reality proper qua reality; it is the moment through which I intellectively know that I am a person. But there is a second moment which constitutes not so much a mode of reality as a modulation, a mode of that mode of reality; it is what I call 'personality', as opposed to merely being a person, which I call 'personeity'. Thus, for example, I can say that a person is a good or bad person, because he really

[33] Ibid., p. 259.

> has this or that set of qualities which modalize his personality. To intellectively know this it does not suffice to point out that now he acted well, or that now he does not give in to temptations. It is necessary to transcend the order of actions and even temptations, in order to go to the mode by which he is, ultimately, this person. This is something which I need to investigate.[34]

By what measure or standard is the observer a person? It is not about a certain set of qualities that I possess or do not possess. It is not even about whether I act this way or that. We have to transcend both the order of characteristics and the order of actions in order to "go to the mode" by which I attain my personhood. What is this mode? Whence do I derive myself? The point is that we are deluded by personality; in actuality the personality rises out of a vast impersonality, individuated out of a background to which the personality itself has no direct access, but materializes due to complex forces. It is sometimes referred to as collective unconscious or mythic archetypes or something else. Be that as it may, the point here is that it is a mode of becoming and not something fixed. We can become relatively fixed due to inertial tendencies, but at core the so-called personality is evolving out of itself, an endless becoming that is a mode, a manner, a method rather than anything else. It is this mode that is of interest rather than its specific expressions. The machine has no mode of becoming; the so-called deep learning systems are nothing but expresseds of an anterior state. Human becoming is not dependent on learning, in fact, the learning itself is a kind of peculiarity of a specific evolutionary circumstance and not its essence.

> St. Augustine had said, *quaestio mihi factus sum*, I have become a question for myself. For this knowledge I need a method, a way that in the reality in which I already am, I am led to my own formal in-depth reality in a physical probing of my own reality. We are dealing with a way by which I achieve, in myself, the discernment of some modalities of reality as opposed to others. This is achieved in the physical probing of my own reality, in an experience of myself. As the probing that it is, this experience consists in an insertion, into my own reality, of a sketch of possibilities (perhaps of something unreal) of what I am. The experience of myself is a knowledge of myself. The idea that experience of myself as a mode of reality consists simply in a type of report or examination of myself is chimerical. By intrinsic necessity, every examination of myself is oriented and inscribed in a system of reference.

[34] Ibid.

> When one speaks of a confession of himself, the concept of confession is not necessarily univocal. What St. Augustine understood by confession is not the same as what Rousseau understood by it. For St. Augustine, to confess to oneself is to know, to have an experience of what I am in my in-depth reality with respect to a very precise system of reference, viz. the reference to what God has realized in me and I in God. On the other hand, for Rousseau, confession is the knowledge of what I am "naturally"; the system of reference is now nature. God and nature are here two systems of reference among many others, without which there could never be any confession. This system of reference leads to a sketch of what I ultimately am. For example, it might be the sketch of a certain vocation: Do I or do I not have that vocation? For this I need to probe the insertion of this sketch (in the foregoing example, of this vocation) into my own reality. Ultimately there is no more than a single physical probing of this insertion, viz. trying to conduct myself by intimately appropriating what has been sketched.[35]

My phenomenological reality must be probed by interpellation of specific sketches of possibilities into my reality in order to find out what resonates with me and what does not. That would be the system of reference by which I unearth the orientation that I have come to know generally as myself. Let us say, I start teaching math and feel that I have found my vocation in it. Now what constitutes finding my vocation? It would perhaps include finding a certain peace and significance in mathematical relationships and in their pedagogical communication. It might also include seeing close parallels between reality and mathematical forms. It might include the ability to rotate and transform mathematical objects inwardly and then being able to communicate that effectively with others. This mathematization of the world of real objects and relationships constitutes my system or field of reference by means of which I discover myself. This discovery, while it is neither absolute nor unchanging, must be probed intimately in order for it to reveal my relationship with what has been sketched and whether there is any substance in it.

> There is no abstract "know thyself"; I can only know myself along the lines of this or that sketch of my own possibilities. Only the sketch of what I "might be" inserted into me as self-appropriation, only this constitutes the form of knowing oneself. Clearly, it is an appropriation in the order of actualization of my own reality. This discernment of oneself is a difficult

[35] Ibid., p. 264.

> operation; it is discernment in probing and self-appropriation. In summary, then, there are four fundamental modes of experience: experimentation, compenetration, verification, and appropriation. They are not methods like the physical, psychological, sociological, historical, and other "methods"; rather, they are modes of methodic intellection, i.e. modes by which we intellectively know, by means of a way, the real, regardless of what the "methods" may be in the usual sense of the word. Every "method" can imply various of these "modes". The unity of the modes is not, then, the unity of "a" method, but something more radical and fundamental, viz. the unity of experience. In virtue of it we say that men have much or little experience, i.e., that they have realized, to a different degree, the physical probing of what reality ultimately is. With this we have examined the two primary moments of the structure of knowing: objectualization and method. It is now necessary to tackle the more important theme relating to our problem: the truth of our knowledge of the depths of the real.[36]

By means of an inquiry into the method of intellection we are able to open up a systematic angle into the ontological distinction between organic or sentient intelligence and machinic cognition. We can see that the latter does not consist of the *experience* of anything; it can only proceed along the logical mode of information processing. But the truth of logic is not the truth of reality, even if it may consist of a facet of the latter. Only sentient intelligence can experience reality, and this experiencing consists at the very least of four distinct modes, namely, orientation, compenetration, corroboration, and interpellation. Let me illustrate these four modal moments by means of an example. Consider a scientist. Looking through biographies of scientists we find innumerable initiating moments or sketches that opened up for them a way of thinking about reality. For example, think of Einstein's famous childhood question of what would happen if one were to ride atop a light wave. In his *Autobiographical Notes*, Einstein wrote about "a paradox upon which I had already hit at the age of sixteen: If I pursue a beam of light with the velocity c (velocity of light in a vacuum), I should observe such a beam of light as an electromagnetic field at rest though spatially oscillating. There seems to be no such thing, however, neither on the basis of experience nor according to Maxwell's equations. From the very beginning it appeared to me intuitively clear that, judged from the standpoint of such an observer, everything would have to happen according to the same laws as for an observer who, relative

[36] Ibid., p. 266.

to the earth, was at rest. For how should the first observer know or be able to determine, that he is in a state of fast uniform motion?"[37] It is arguable as to whether this sketch or thought experiment later led to Einstein's famous discoveries on the electrodynamics of moving bodies or to relativity theory, but what is indisputable is that this sketch constituted a serious mode of experience. Einstein speaks of the process and significance of what we have called sketch-making in the following manner:

> When, at the reception of sense-impressions, memory-pictures emerge, this is not yet "thinking." And when such pictures form series, each member of which calls forth another, this, too, is not yet "thinking." When, however, a certain picture turns up in many such series, then—precisely through such return—it becomes an ordering element for such series, in that it connects series which in themselves are unconnected. Such an element becomes an instrument, a concept- I think that the transition from free association or "dreaming" to thinking is characterized by the more or less dominating role which the "concept" plays in it. It is by no means necessary that a concept must be connected with a sensorily cognizable and reproducible sign (word); but when this is the case thinking becomes by means of that fact communicable. With what right—the reader will ask—does this man operate so carelessly and primitively with ideas in such a problematic realm without making even the least effort to prove anything? My defense is that all our thinking is of this nature of a free play with concepts; the justification for this play lies in the measure of survey over the experience of the senses which we are able to achieve with its aid. The concept of "truth" cannot yet be applied to such a structure; to my thinking this concept can come in question only when a far-reaching agreement (convention) concerning the elements and rules of the game is already at hand. For me it is not dubious that our thinking goes on for the most part without use of signs (words) and beyond that to a considerable degree unconsciously. For how, otherwise, should it happen that sometimes we "wonder" quite spontaneously about some experience? This "wondering" seems to occur when an experience comes into conflict with a world of concepts which is already sufficiently fixed in us. Whenever such a conflict is experienced hard and intensively it reacts back upon our thought world in a decisive way. The development of this thought world is in a certain sense a continuous flight of "wonder."[38]

[37] Albert Einstein, *Notes for an Autobiography*, https://archive.org/stream/EinsteinAutobiography_djvu.txt.

[38] Ibid.

The words of the philosopher-scientist brilliantly capture the essential process of sketching which provides an orientation to intelligent seeking. Einstein speaks of the "free play with concepts" and its justification lying in the "experience of the senses." The sketch or this free play is rather a "measure of survey" and even a "flight of wonder" that often occur subliminally without the use of linguistic signs. This assertion is of great significance for our argument setting apart sentient intelligence from any simulation of the expressed. But to go ahead with the nature of experience, from Einstein's "confessions" we are able to deduce what has been described as a moment of compenetration.

> The essential in the being of a man of my type lies precisely in what he thinks and how he thinks, not in what he does or suffers. Consequently, the [autobiography] can limit itself in the main to the communicating of thoughts which have played a considerable role in my endeavors. A theory is the more impressive the greater the simplicity of its premises is, the more different kinds of things it relates, and the more extended is its area of applicability. Therefore the deep impression which classical thermodynamics made upon me. It is the only physical theory of universal content concerning which I am convinced that, within the framework of the applicability of its basic concepts, it will never be overthrown (for the special attention of those who are skeptics on principle). The most fascinating subject at the time that I was a student was Maxwell's theory. What made this theory appear revolutionary was the transition from forces at a distance to fields as fundamental variables. The incorporation of optics into the theory of electromagnetism, with its relation of the speed of light to the electric and magnetic absolute system of units as well as the relation of the refraction coefficient to the dielectric constant, the qualitative relation between the reflection coefficient and the metallic conductivity of the body—*it was like a revelation.*[39]

I will begin with the last sentence: "it was like a revelation." A person of Einstein's mental acuteness would not use words like revelation that has theological overtones casually. But what is revelation? The *Book of Revelation* or the *Book of the Apocalypse* is the final book of the New Testament. Written in Koine Greek, its title is derived from the first word

[39] Ibid. Italics mine.

of the text: apokalypsis, meaning "unveiling" or "revelation."[40] Its author is someone who refers to himself as John. So, what does it mean to say it was *like* a revelation. The latter is the experience of a revealment of that which is to come. It is the flashment of a future that has already occurred. When the veil of ignorance is lifted by Grace, there is an apocalyptic moment in which we come to be in the blinding presence of Truth. Einstein experienced a kind of religious moment in his contact with cer-

[40] From the *Book of Revelation* of the New Testament: "Then I saw in the right hand of him who sat on the throne a scroll with writing on both sides and sealed with seven seals. And I saw a mighty angel proclaiming in a loud voice, "Who is worthy to break the seals and open the scroll?" But no one in heaven or on earth or under the earth could open the scroll or even look inside it. I wept and wept because no one was found who was worthy to open the scroll or look inside. Then one of the elders said to me, "Do not weep! See, the Lion of the tribe of Judah, the Root of David, has triumphed. He is able to open the scroll and its seven seals." Then I saw a Lamb, looking as if it had been slain, standing at the center of the throne, encircled by the four living creatures and the elders. The Lamb had seven horns and seven eyes, which are the seven spirits of God sent out into all the earth. He went and took the scroll from the right hand of him who sat on the throne. And when he had taken it, the four living creatures and the twenty-four elders fell down before the Lamb. Each one had a harp and they were holding golden bowls full of incense, which are the prayers of God's people. And they sang a new song, saying:

> You are worthy to take the scroll
>   and to open its seals,
> because you were slain,
>   and with your blood you purchased for God
>   persons from every tribe and language and people and nation.
> You have made them to be a kingdom and priests to serve our God,
>   and they will reign on the earth.

Then I looked and heard the voice of many angels, numbering thousands upon thousands, and ten thousand times ten thousand. They encircled the throne and the living creatures and the elders. In a loud voice they were saying:

> Worthy is the Lamb, who was slain,
> to receive power and wealth and wisdom and strength
> and honor and glory and praise!

Then I heard every creature in heaven and on earth and under the earth and on the sea, and all that is in them, saying:

> To him who sits on the throne and to the Lamb
> be praise and honor and glory and power,
> for ever and ever!

tain theories of physics that seemed to him to be essential. It is the understanding of this "qualitative relation" between optics and electrodynamics that produces in Einstein the compenetration of the conceptual and the phenomenological. It is a transformative moment that sets up his future trajectory as a scientist. From here, Einstein will seek out the ground of reality along these lines of rational intellection using this reference system.

Finally, we are at the point of verification. Here the rational intellection uses the system of reference to verify for oneself the sketch of what one is actually. From an earlier paragraph, we see that it might be the sketch of a certain vocation: "Do I or do I not have that vocation? For this I need to probe the insertion of this sketch into my own reality." In the case of Einstein, the philosopher-scientist grows into the domain of original thinkers in science through an insight into the nature of inertial systems.

> According to the rules of connection, used in classical physics, of the spatial coordinates and of the time of events in the transition from one inertial system to another the two assumptions of (1) the constancy of the light velocity and (2) the independence of the laws (thus specially also of the law of the constancy of the light velocity) of the choice of the inertial system (principle of special relativity) are mutually incompatible (despite the fact that both taken separately are based on experience). The insight which is fundamental for the special theory of relativity is this: the assumptions (1) and (2) are compatible if relations of a new type ("Lorentz- transformation") are postulated for the conversion of coordinates and the times of events. With the given physical interpretation of coordinates and time, this is by no means merely a conventional step, but implies certain hypotheses concerning the actual behavior of moving measuring-rods and clocks, which can be experimentally validated or disproved. The universal principle of the special theory of relativity is contained in the postulate: the laws of physics are invariant with respect to the Lorentz-transformations (for the transition from one inertial system to any other arbitrarily chosen system of inertia). This is a restricting principle for natural laws, comparable to the restricting principle of the non-existence of the perpetuum mobile which underlies thermodynamics.[41]

[41] Ibid.

By his own account, Einstein's understanding of himself was fundamentally formed out of the concepts and ideas he was involved with and nothing else. So his verification of who he was necessarily involved the rarefied concepts he mulled over within himself, and we generally mull over those concepts which come in conflict with the established beliefs around us. It is clear from the above passage that the core principle around which Einstein's consciousness evolved in rational intellection was the invariance principle. His being is verified by resonance with the restricting principle within natural laws that regulates translation between inertial systems. In fact, Relativity Theory is a misnomer. There is nothing remotely relativistic in Einstein's thought. His system of reference is invariance and he came to be defined by it. "God does not play dice" was his sardonic comment when he was first presented with the probabilistic model of subatomic phenomena. Deeply religious but with no allegiance to formal religion, Einstein's life presents a study in the different modes of experience afforded to the sentient, being almost a ridiculously appropriate illustration of the distinctions of which we have been speaking thus far. We will see more of this great intelligence in Chap. 3, where we find him in conversation with another prodigious scientific mind, Werner Heisenberg. Listening to their exchange, we are filled with a sense of Presence that is worlds apart from the technofantasies about superintelligent machines and other related ideas about the future of the species. It might appear as though we are unnecessarily drawing a comparison between unrelated domains, but are we? In drawing a comparison between the scientific spirit and the technological attitude, we come upon something important. The former, as we shall see in the coming pages, is imbued with true inquiry into the unknown, whereas the latter borders on technodeterminism and algorithmic triumphalism. The former fills one with hope in the human spirit, whereas the latter is laced with a kind of dystopic materialism. The first is helpful in the bringing forth of sentient potentiality, whereas the second is keen on displacement and prosthesis. A pedagogy of poiesis is warranted in such circumstances, for otherwise we have the situation of the *One Dimensional Man* of Herbert Marcuse, who wrote about the comfortable and smooth "democratic unfreedom" of modern technocratic totalitarianism and narcissism.

CHAPTER 3

The Ghost in the Machine

The attitude of modernist educators seem to reflect a conscious or unconscious belief that a mind-brain stuffed with knowledge is a wonderful platform for actualizing human potential and becoming intelligent. Hence, in the race and eagerness to pack it with as much information and algorithmic capabilities as possible—the more the better—the general aim of education has come to rest on maximizing algorithmic and data-based learning. This attitude inevitably opens the door for infiltration by Artificial Intelligence enthusiasts in education, who sincerely believe that AI is here to do education a favor. The educational space becomes thick with AI talk and how it might be the future of learning because we will learn from machines and the way they learn, and so on. Without doubt there is a larger epistemic in the background, a fundamental belief underlying modernity, which is that life and existence are puzzles to be solved. This puzzle, like all puzzles, has various pieces, and these can be brought together eventually to complete the reality picture. Our education system has inherited this representation of reality and organized itself, albeit at a much-diluted level, along these lines. Although it must be admitted that, of late, this puzzle-view of reality has stumbled and partly fallen from grace, and the cognoscenti no longer believe in this theory. Nevertheless, the momentum of the past is such that in most important areas such as education the epistemic of the past continues to hold its sway over the social imaginary. The consequence is that symbolic learning takes

K. Roy, *Education, "Artificial" Intelligence, and Cognition*,
https://doi.org/10.1007/978-3-031-82263-6_3

complete precedence over phenomenological education. In other words, we give much more importance to monologic and one-sided loading of the human brain than allowing it to engage in debate and dialogue. The model is acquisition rather than awakening.

What I intend to do in this chapter is to highlight, by means of discourse and content analysis, the dialogic exchanges between certain scientists, who were beginning to emerge as notable thinkers in their respective fields, in order to better understand the thinking by which they progressed. The breathless power of these dialogues would make it clear to even die-hard supporters of AI in education as to why human intelligence has little to do with machinic capacities other than being able to program and use them as glorified computing machines or speedy search engines. It is my submission that toying with AI ideas as though they were somehow approximations of conscious intelligence or are potential replacement for general human intelligence severely detracts from the growth of young minds as critical and creative thinkers independent of the contagion of AI-related discourse. The work and purpose of the two kinds of capacities—sentient intelligence and AI—are qualitatively different, belonging to two different ontological orders. A compilation of court cases is not a legal argument, a literature review is not a novel, a set of affordances or efficiencies is not the physics problem, an extensive collection of rhythms and meters is not poetry, and so on. One could give countless examples that show why the current hyper buzz around AI is hype, even motivated hype, and nothing else, that, if taken seriously, might lead to the not-yet-mature becoming even more deprived and deluded. When the hype begins to fade, the folks who will be left holding the simulacra will surely be those who had taken the frenzy to be toward something real, while the actual existential issues lay in the psycho-somatic and eco-organic rather than in the informational and the algorithmic. For instance, the experience of problems like depression or alienation or unfeelingness as existential states cannot be digitalized even if its subsequent investigation may involve advanced diagnostics. Nor are the obverse side to these issues, such as being engaged or feeling creative, have any artificial correlates. Attempting to seek digital simulation in intellectual pursuits leads to a sterile mindscape in which the unwary risk being stranded. The reason for laboring the point here is because too much is being made of AI and machine learning currently, including painting scenarios that connect it to the future of education, and even to that of humanity itself. It is important to be properly educated about the distinct ontologies and of the consequences of confounding these without being alarmist.

The passages presented for analysis below are from an extended period of intellectual contact between two of the leading lights of twentieth-century physics, namely, Werner Heisenberg and Albert Einstein. What follows is an extraordinary dialogue in which the two leading scientists—one established and the other emerging—disagree about almost everything including the nature of reality and the meaning of scientific description. What is remarkable is the manner in which they dig in their heels in their respective positions and raise fundamental questions in ontology and epistemology through their scientific dispute, without ever questioning the depth and weight of each other's positions. These questions and debates have since become scientific folklore, and helped shape the thinking of a generation of scientific workers. The reason I include this here is to present a glimpse of the *intelligent labor of meaning making* apparent in the scientists' dialogues as evidenced in their admissions and arguments. The brief biographical sketches show the relentless search for truth as a way of being in the world that is not circumscribed by mechanical capabilities. What is visible more than anything else in the following lines is the *aesthetic aspect* of human understanding; that is, poiesis rather than techne, although they are debating about the nature of the material world.

Reminiscing about the early moments of his pathbreaking theory Heisenberg writes:

> I concentrated on demonstrating that the conservation law held [for my theory], and one evening I reached the point where I was ready to determine the individual terms in the energy table, or, as we put it today, in the energy matrix, by what would now be considered an extremely clumsy series of calculations. When the first terms seemed to accord with the energy principle, I became rather excited, and I began to make countless arithmetical errors. As a result, it was almost three o'clock in the morning before the final result of my computations lay before me. The energy principle had held for all the terms, and I could no longer doubt the mathematical consistency and coherence of the kind of quantum mechanics to which my calculations pointed. At first, I was deeply alarmed. I had the feeling that, through the surface of atomic phenomena, I was looking at a strangely beautiful interior, and felt almost giddy at the thought that I now had to probe this wealth of mathematical structures nature had so generously spread out before me. I was far too excited to sleep, and so, as a new day dawned, I made for the

> southern tip of the island, where I had been longing to climb a rock jutting out into the sea. I now did so without too much trouble, and waited for the sun to rise.[1]

The opening point to note is that Heisenberg did not reach his theoretical conclusions through mere calculations. It is clarified elsewhere that "Heisenberg conducted a thought experiment. … He considered trying to measure the position of an electron with a gamma ray microscope. The high-energy photon used to illuminate the electron would give it a kick, changing its momentum in an uncertain way. A higher resolution microscope would require higher energy light, giving an even bigger kick to the electron. The more precisely one tried to measure the position, the more uncertain the momentum would become, and vice versa, Heisenberg reasoned. This uncertainty is a fundamental feature of quantum mechanics, not a limitation of any particular experimental apparatus."[2] This thought experiment reveals thinking at two levels—one, at the level of ordinary experience wherein there are atoms, and gamma rays that illuminate and give it a kick, just as though we were in a football field with players kicking around a ball. This naïve level of mental representation is quite shocking when you think we are talking about sub-atomic reality, and yet such naïve imagery is employed by none other than Heisenberg. At the same time, at another level, there *is* the realization that the electron is *not* a football, and the very seeking of information about it will end up interfering with the part reality, in a way that it does not happen to footballs. This double layered thinking, sometimes called complementarity, is a mode of human genius that can create multi-level scenarios checking upon each successively by the other levels. It illustrates what it means to think beyond ordinary chatter, but it also shows quite clearly why no pre-meditated programming or execution of algorithm can do this kind of thinking. For that would require the programmer to know what to think in advance. But for the programmer or algorithm to know what to think or even how to think in this case, s/he has to have the inspired genius of Heisenberg that determines the direction of thought and its problematization. Hence, the first difference of embodied intelligence is intuitive insight and not computational skill.

[1] Werner Heisenberg, *Physics and Beyond*, p. 61.

[2] David Cassidy, *Uncertainty: The Life and Science of Werner Heisenberg* (New York: W.H. Freeman, 1992).

Heisenberg continues with his narrative and brings us to the important juncture at which he presents his ideas before Albert Einstein who is already a byword in Physics at the time of the encounter.

> I apparently managed to arouse Einstein's interest, for he invited me to walk home with him so that we might discuss the new ideas at greater length. On the way, he asked about my studies and previous research. As soon as we were indoors, he opened the conversation with a question that bore on the philosophical background of my recent work. "What you have told us sounds extremely strange. You assume the existence of electrons inside the atom, and you are probably quite right to do so. But you refuse to consider their orbits, even though we can observe electron tracks in a cloud chamber. I should very much like to hear more about your reasons for making such strange assumptions." "We cannot observe electron orbits inside the atom," I replied, "but the radiation which an atom emits during discharges enables us to deduce the frequencies and corresponding amplitudes of its electrons. After all, even in the older physics wave numbers and amplitudes could be considered substitutes for electron orbits. Now, since a good theory must be based on directly observable magnitudes, I thought it more fitting to restrict myself to these, treating them, as it were, as representatives of the electron orbits."[3]

Heisenberg's theory had refused to consider electron orbits without rejecting the existence of the electron itself inside the atom. Einstein was quick to pick up on this point and pressed Heisenberg for the logic of his approach. Yet what does it mean for an electron or its orbits to "exist?" Can we speak of the existence of evanescents that cannot even withstand being "observed"? For observation conventionally implies a movement of information between the observer and the target, but the problem lies in the fact that in the case of evanescents the information carrier (some kind of radiation) itself is much more unwieldy relative to the observed (like an elephant attempting to convey information about an ant, to put it crudely). Therefore, precisely at what point can we say that existence as we know comes to be? And, where are the discontinuities in natural ways of expression when we come to understanding scientific phenomena? Can intelligence communicate between these levels? These kinds of questions have not been settled but have instead been brushed aside due to practical reasons, but these questions are immensely important from an educational

[3] Heisenberg, op. cit., p. 62.

point of view because it reveals the strangeness of the world we inhabit. Dialogues about the strangeness are not idle discussions but are the flesh and blood of new discoveries. So, the second difference of embodied intelligence is being in a delicate relationship with the Unknown filled with aporia.

As the conversation progresses, the two scientists begin to discuss about fundamentals. And in the lines that follow, Einstein makes one of those stunning sage-like statements that has remained burning like a beacon in the intellectual life of the species.

> "But you don't seriously believe," Einstein protested, "that none but observable magnitudes must go into a physical theory?" "Isn't that precisely what you have done with relativity?" I asked in some surprise. "After all, you did stress the fact that it is impermissible to speak of absolute time, simply because absolute time cannot be observed; that only clock readings, be it in the moving reference system or the system at rest, are relevant to the determination of time." "Possibly I did use this kind of reasoning," Einstein admitted, "but it is nonsense all the same. Perhaps I could put it more diplomatically by saying that it may be heuristically useful to keep in mind what one has actually observed. But on principle, it is quite wrong to try founding a theory on observable magnitudes alone. In reality the very opposite happens. It is the theory which decides what we can observe. You must appreciate that observation is a very complicated process. The phenomenon under observation produces certain events in our measuring apparatus. As a result, further processes take place in the apparatus, which eventually and by complicated paths produce sense impressions and help us to fix the effects in our consciousness. Along this whole path-from the phenomenon to its fixation in our consciousness-we must be able to tell how nature functions, must know the natural laws at least in practical terms, before we can claim to have observed anything at all. Only theory, that is, knowledge of natural laws, enables us to deduce the underlying phenomena from our sense impressions.[4]

What is the relation between theory and observation? Further, what is the connection of this relation to intelligence? When we *speak about* intelligence, is it from observation or from theory? Schoolchildren are often taught that science begins with observation and experiment, but Einstein makes that famous statement to the contrary, one that has been quoted ever since—"It is the theory that decides what we can observe." Also, in

[4] Ibid., p. 63.

saying that "observation is a complicated process," Einstein makes yet another great admission. Taken together, these give a profound metaphysics of science. Theory is a specific relation to a part reality, that gives rise to a formalism. The latter is a manner of resonance between an entity/group and what we call the physical world. If science is ultimately based on this resonance, that is to say, if what we can observe or our direction of observation is based on a formalism, then the intelligent activity called science cannot be separated from the intelligence of intuition. No human activity including science can be independent of the intuitive resonance by which we make primary contact with the world, and from which arise our beliefs about the world. These beliefs are continually modified through observation and discussion, but they remain about a part reality, and are always approximations, no matter how useful. Given that context, Einstein is dead-on when he says that it is the theory that decides what we can observe. There is no such thing as observation that is independent of a selection system and a corresponding symbolic universe set up uniquely through resonance with the world. Thus we come upon the third difference of embodied intelligence: Complementarity and simultaneous multilevel thinking that proceed by means of resonance.

But to continue with the narrative:

> I was completely taken aback by Einstein's attitude, though I found his arguments convincing. Hence I said: "The idea that a good theory is no more than a condensation of observations in accordance with the principle of thought economy surely goes back to Mach, and it has, in fact, been said that your relativity theory makes decisive use of Machian concepts. But what you have just told me seems to indicate the very opposite. What am I to make of all this, or rather what do you yourself think about it?" "I consider Mach's concept of observation also much too naive. He pretends that we know perfectly well what the word 'observe' means, and thinks this exempts him from having to discriminate between 'objective' and 'subjective' phenomena. No wonder his principle has so suspiciously commercial a name: 'thought economy.' His idea of simplicity is much too subjective for me. In reality, the simplicity of natural laws is an objective fact as well, and the correct conceptual scheme must balance the subjective side of this simplicity with the objective. But that is a very difficult task. Let us rather return to your lecture. I have a strong suspicion that, precisely because of the problems we have just been discussing, your theory will one day get you into hot water. I should like to explain this in greater detail. When it comes to observation, you behave as if everything can be left as it was, that is, as if you

> could use the old descriptive language. In that case, however, you will also have to say: in a cloud chamber we can observe the path of the electrons. At the same time, you claim that there are no electron paths inside the atom. This is obvious nonsense, for you cannot possibly get rid of the path simply by restricting the space in which the electron moves."[5]

Is a good theory to be framed in terms of thought economy? If so, then it implies that a theory is not a direct description of "what is," but is mediated by an additional principle of intellectual brevity. Besides, what are we to make of Einstein's assertion that "the correct conceptual scheme must balance the subjective side with the objective?" Is this not yet another mediation and not merely a revealment? But first let us see what Mach means by economy in his typology in the *Economy of Science*:

> One can identify ten elements in *The Development of Mechanics* relevant to the economy of science. The elements on the left-hand side of the following chart, the "methods," are ways to promote the economy of science. The elements on the right-hand side, the "effects," are results of employing these methods.

Methods that Promote Economy	**The Effects of These Methods**
"Instinctive knowledge"	Transparency
The method of differences	Empirical fruitfulness
The law of continuity of experience	The ability to disregard details
Relations of the whole	Computational power
	Minimization
	Completion of experience

> Computational power, according to this chart, should be seen not (just) as an absolute property of a principle of science, but as the result of employing an economical method. One example of an economical method is the "method of differences", which Mach discusses in his lecture "On the Conservation of Energy". Experience teaches us that some sensed elements of the world are interdependent—pressure, volume, and heat in a gas, for example. But there are differences as well as dependence. Theories should be analyzed in terms of their observable "elements". The goal of science is to show that some elements of a theory (variables such as pressure and volume) are dependent on other elements of the theory (variables such as motion and density). To show that the independent group is smaller than

[5] Ibid., p. 66.

the dependent group is to promote economy in science. Mach calls this the "method of differences".[6]

Mach's characterization that computational power is not an absolute property, but is the consequence of a specific method of scientific economy, is a very significant statement. It is an incredible admission that computational power, which has become central to modern science, even a substitute in some cases, is in actuality incidental, and not a mode of absolute revealment. Those familiar with present-day science will know the extent to which the sciences are dependent on calculations. In fact, physicists today are not able to give a description of the phenomena under study in normal language, but increasingly depend upon the results of their calculations, indirectly inferring from these ("efficiencies" and "affordances") what is going on. The implication may be that science is another truth game and not an absolute correspondence with reality anymore. Although this may not have been Mach's or Einstein's viewpoint or intent, the interesting gap between their respective positions certainly press us in this direction. And from this we derive the fourth difference of embodied intelligence: Authentic difference, or the difference authored by aesthetic preferences of grouping such as dependent/independent. No machine can make these decisions because these are aesthetic distinctions connected to the elegance of a theory, and have nothing to do with algorithms or calculations. This does not mean, however, that such a characterization leans toward the arbitrary. The aesthetic of elegance is neither arbitrary nor whimsical, but lies in the fine balance of a delicate empiricism, and reveals more by that virtue, than the purely objective or the purely subjective.

Let us continue with the dialogue between the two pathbreaking scientists:

> I tried to come to the defense of the new quantum mechanics. "For the time being, we have no idea in what language we must speak about processes inside the atom. True, we have a mathematical language, that is, a mathematical scheme for determining the stationary states of the atom or the transition probabilities from one state to another, but we do not know-at

[6] Lydia Patton, "New Water in Old Buckets: Hypothetical and Counterfactual Reasoning in Mach's Economy of Science," In *Ernst Mach—Life, Work, and Influence/Ernst Mach—Leben, Werk und Wirkung,* ed./hg. Friedrich Stadler (Dordrecht: Vienna Circle Institute Yearbook, Springer 2019).

least not in general-how this language is related to that of classical physics. And, of course, we need this connection if we are to apply this theory to experiments in the first place. For when it comes to experiments, we invariably speak in the traditional language. Hence I cannot really claim that we have 'understood' quantum mechanics. I assume that the mathematical scheme works, but no link with the traditional language has been established so far. And until that has been done, we cannot hope to speak of the path of the electron in the cloud chamber without inner contradictions. Hence it is probably much too early to solve the difficulties you have mentioned."[7]

At the level of experiments, wherein a certain description must be assumed about what the experiment is all about, scientists use everyday language or the language of classical physics, as we have seen earlier. But beyond that in carrying out procedures, this language is replaced by mathematical schemas, probabilities, quantum states, and so on, none of which are translatable into ordinary language. Heisenberg points out this fundamental difficulty in speaking about sub-atomic phenomena due to the chasm between the language of reality and the mathematics. And if understanding means being able to grasp the mathematics in terms of mental representations or imagery, no such understanding has emerged even to this day, let alone at the time of Heisenberg when the new physics was beginning to emerge. To Heisenberg's pleading his case, Einstein gives this memorable reply:

"Very well, I will accept that," Einstein said. "We shall talk about it again in a few years' time. But perhaps I may put another question to you. Quantum theory as you have expounded it in your lecture has two distinct faces. On the one hand, as Bohr himself has rightly stressed, it explains the stability of the atom; it causes the same forms to reappear time and again. On the other hand, it explains that strange discontinuity or inconstancy of nature which we observe quite clearly when we watch flashes of light on a scintillation screen. These two aspects are obviously connected. In your quantum mechanics you will have to take both into account, for instance when you speak of the emission of light by atoms. You can calculate the discrete energy values of the stationary states. Your theory can thus account for the stability of certain forms that cannot merge continuously into one another, but must differ by finite amounts and seem capable of permanent reformation. But what happens during the emission of light? As you know, I suggested that, when an atom drops suddenly from one stationary energy value to the next,

[7] Heisenberg op. cit., p. 66.

it emits the energy difference as an energy packet, a so-called light quantum. In that case, we have a particularly clear example of discontinuity. Do you think that my conception is correct? Or can you describe the transition from one stationary state to another in a more precise way?" (67)

Einstein observes that Bohr's model of the atom and Heisenberg's quantum mechanics are consistent with the fact of stability of the atomic structure as well as with the strange discontinuities that occur when electrons jump about in their orbits giving off radiation. The calculations are consistent with both faces of the theory. However, what was not known was *what happens in between*. Of course, it is possible to argue that this business of "what happens in between" is a conventional superstition, because in everyday life, there is always something in between when we transition from one state to another. But there may not be anything in atomic or sub-atomic reality which is parallel to it. Therefore, there is nothing amiss in the theory, but only in our conditioned expectations from being in the natural state. Nevertheless, the struggle to mentally grasp the strangeness of elements changing states without going through any intermediate states is enough to send the thinker into a phenomenological tailspin, something the machine cannot know anything about. From our perspective, we can draw the distinction of negation, that is, of being able to grasp conventional experience not as something absolute but the product of a certain level (of reality).

In my reply, I said something like this: "Bohr has taught me that one cannot describe this process by means of the traditional concepts, i.e., as a process in time and space. With that, of course, we have said very little, no more, in fact, than that we do not know. Whether or not I should believe in light quanta, I cannot say at this stage. Radiation quite obviously involves the discontinuous elements to which you refer as light quanta. On the other hand, there is a continuous element, which appears, for instance, in interference phenomena, and which is much more simply described by the wave theory of light. But you are of course quite right to ask whether quantum mechanics has anything new to say on these terribly difficult problems. I believe that we may at least hope that it will one day.[8]

That there are things that happen outside normal time and space is not new to mysticism and esoteric doctrines. But logical positivists,

[8] Ibid., p. 67.

empiricists, and scientists in general have always sneered at such claims, dismissing them as hallucinations or innocent delusions. However, if the statement of a highly competent scientist that there are things that cannot be described "as a process in time and space" is to be taken seriously, then that brings scientific reality breathtakingly close to that esoteric creativity through which an alternate and complementary reality has been traditionally expressed. This is not to promote irresponsible esotericism, or glorify vulgar occultism, but to highlight the fact that the frontiers of knowledge present a different kind of challenge to thought, and for which a very different kind of creative intelligence is required beyond sophisticated algorithms and elaborate calculations. Here we need the capacity to carry on an inner dialogue with oneself with a single-minded intent to overcome the bounds of one's own thinking that can help in going beyond the aporia. This is indeed risky, for one can stand accused of solipsistic idealism.

> "You are moving on very thin ice," Einstein warned me. "For you are suddenly speaking of what we know about nature and no longer about what nature really does. In science we ought to be concerned solely with what nature does. It might very well be that you and I know quite different things about nature. But who would be interested in that? Perhaps you and I alone. To everyone else it is a matter of complete indifference. In other words, if your theory is right, you will have to tell me sooner or later what the atom does when it passes from one stationary state to the next."[9]

Throughout his career, Einstein continued to hold the belief that we can know about "what nature really does," rather than our epistemic constructs of it, and the job of science was to figure out this absolute ontology. Now, this question about how things actually are, as distinct from how we perceive them to be, is almost as ancient as philosophy itself. It has been an unresolved question as to whether, from being within and part of natural processes, we can objectively know what nature does. Also, it is part of the puzzle as to exactly where do we draw the line between the observer and the observed so as to be able to claim that an absolutely authentic ontological observation has been made. Is such a separation even theoretically possible, and can we simply rely on our senses and thought for synthesis, or is all mapping of the cosmos just one game of truth among many? For instance, relativists would say that just because we

[9] Ibid., p. 68.

are constituted of volume, heat, and pressure, we find these absolutes in the world around us. If these were not our physical determinants, then we would have found quite different measures to understand the world around us. Hence, for the relativist, phenomenological projection is an inevitable part of everything we do, including science.

But the question of technology is a little different, being at once-remove from its parent—scientific inquiry. The typical technologist does not entertain these doubts because of the stability and reliability that technological measurements offer. But technology does not pretend to tell us anything about the world, only about observed changes in matter due to manifold interventions. The difficulty lies when an individual changes frames from science to technology or mixes up the frames without understanding or acknowledging it. Artificial intelligence is born of such a mix up. Questions of intelligence belong to science, whereas problems of mimicking, simulation, cloning, and synthetic and artificial production are issues and methods of technology. In other words, artificial anything points to copying, whereas intelligence is ongoing creation. The former relates to recreating the dead past, whereas the latter refers to the not-yet, or to creative emergence. Creative emergence cannot be copied, only its remains can be examined post mortem, and pieced together like a fossil. Artificial intelligence, no matter how successful in algorithmic calculations, is essentially a fossil, unconnected with living intelligence and its struggle to comprehend reality.

> Bohr's discussions with Schrodinger began at the railway station and were continued daily from early morning until late at night. Schrodinger stayed in Bohr's house so that nothing would interrupt the conversations. And although Bohr was normally most considerate and friendly in his dealings with people, he now struck me as an almost remorseless fanatic, one who was not prepared to make the least concession or grant that he could ever be mistaken. It is hardly possible to convey just how passionate the discussions were, just how deeply rooted the convictions of each, a fact that marked their every utterance. All I can hope to do here is to produce a very pale copy of conversations in which two men were fighting for their particular interpretation of the new mathematical scheme with all the powers at their command.[10]

[10] Ibid., p. 73.

What was at stake between Bohr and Schrödinger was what became known as the Copenhagen Interpretation. Bohr, the formulator of the Copenhagen Interpretation, involved denying that particles, orbits, trajectories, and so on had any ultimate meaning at the quantum level. Only probability density distributions had any meaning that apparently collapsed into particles. But Bohr was ultimately unable to convince Schrödinger who came up with his own wave mechanics. What is our point here? It is this: Three great minds, three conscious intelligences were faced toward the Open-Unknown for intimations and inspiration. They were working from the Unknown to the known. Whereas, the artificial works from the known to the known, the organic conscious intelligence stays open with its intuitions, awake for any echo from the unknown.

> Since our talks often continued till long after midnight, and did not produce a satisfactory conclusion despite protracted efforts over several months, both of us became utterly exhausted and rather tense. Hence Bohr decided in February 1927 to go skiing in Norway, and I was quite glad to be left behind in Copenhagen, where I could think about these hopelessly complicated problems undisturbed. I now concentrated all my efforts on the mathematical representation of the electron path in the cloud chamber, and when I realized fairly soon that the obstacles before me were quite insurmountable, I began to wonder whether we might not have been asking the wrong sort of question all along. But where had we gone wrong? The path of the electron through the cloud chamber obviously existed; one could easily observe it. The mathematical framework of quantum mechanics existed as well, and was much too convincing to allow for any changes. Hence it ought to be possible to establish a connection between the two, hard though it appeared to be. It must have been one evening after midnight when I suddenly remembered my conversation with Einstein and particularly his statement, "It is the theory which decides what we can observe." I was immediately convinced that the key to the gate that had been closed for so long must be sought right here. I decided to go on a nocturnal walk through Faelled Park and to think further about the matter.[11]

The question before science is never the discovery of an ultimate reality, for that is the terrain of mystic revelation. The question before scientific intelligence is to find a non-contradictory and consistent path of progress that does not come in conflict with the observable or sensible reality. But

[11] Ibid., p. 77.

science had reached a point in its investigations into nature where none of the classical methods and normal ways of thinking were working. Scientists were being forced to accept a weird and bizarre view of reality that was at conflict with our experience of terra firma. Only the mathematics agreed; but the senses revolted. And this was inevitable, for the senses and our language born of ordinary experience were never meant for describing a sub-atomic reality. Therefore, the problem was not in our natural language system but in assuming that our normal ways of thinking were adequate for all levels of reality. The fact that the level of the hard flesh rested upon not hard certainties but a ghostly sub-atomic game whose description could only be given in abstract mathematical terms irreconcilable with mental representation was hard to swallow for even the greatest of minds. For in this domain, all descriptions, no matter whose version—Bohr's, Heisenberg's, or Schrödinger's—turned out to be equally hazy. And the mathematical description in each case was not an explanation.

> Once again it was driven home to me how terribly difficult it is to give up an attitude on which one's entire scientific approach and career have been based. Einstein had devoted his life to probing into that objective world of physical processes which runs its course in space and time, independent of us, according to firm laws. The mathematical symbols of theoretical physics were also symbols of this objective world and as such enabled physicists to make statements about its future behavior. And now it was being asserted that, on the atomic scale, this objective world of time and space did not even exist and that the mathematical symbols of theoretical physics referred to possibilities rather than to facts. Einstein was not prepared to let us do what, to him, amounted to pulling the ground from under his feet. Later in life, also, when quantum theory had long since become an integral part of modern physics, Einstein was unable to change his attitude-at best, he was prepared to accept the existence of quantum theory as a temporary expedient. "God does not throw dice" was his unshakable principle, one that he would not allow anybody to challenge. To which Bohr could only counter with: "Nor is it our business to prescribe to God how He should run the world."[12]

It is more than difficult—it means giving up a whole way of thinking and being wherein we have come to accept the hard, fleshly reality as the true and only reality. It takes more than one meditation to penetrate into the ghostly reality beneath and come to the realization that what we know

[12] Ibid., pp. 80–81.

as normal reality is nothing other than just one level among many. In other words, there seems to be an ethereality on which our normal reality rests. Please notice that we are referring to an *ethereality* rather than an unreality. Even probability density distributions and so forth are a brave but pathetic way to grasp this ethereality, because these are nevertheless a description from the gross level. It is the fleshly reality trying to second-guess a ghostly reality. Exactly at which point and how the real emerges from the ethereal is not clear and continues to puzzle scientists. To put it in more conventional terms, universals such as volume, pressure, and heat have no meaning at the sub-atomic level, and yet make their appearance somewhere along the way in the transition from the ethereal to the real. Today, even high school students of physics familiar with the basics of quantum theory know about curious sub-atomic phenomena. But what they do not comprehend is the sheer breathtaking improbability of what they assume so naïvely and innocently. This improbability was clear to Einstein and he resisted it furiously. The vast intelligence of the man tried to juxtapose and reconcile the ethereal with the real, and failed. This was no ordinary failure, but a failure of heroic proportions, before which ordinary successes pale into insignificance. In that failure lay the struggle of living consciousness attempting to come to terms with the extravagance of nature that keeps its secrets from its products. This conatus or struggle is the task of living intelligence, and not to be overwhelmed by artificially mimicry or synthetic reproduction of its material substratum, which may be useful for running society, but is useless in understanding the relation of the real to the ethereal. Among other things, an important task of education is precisely to raise these issues in consciousness again and again in different ways, keeping alive the tension between the two levels of reality.

Why are we laboring this point here? It is to resist the AI discourse from hijacking the understanding of intelligence and its ontology, and diverting it into a pre-set channel. While no one can deny the vast changes in practical life that AI is bringing and will further introduce in the times to come, we have to make sure that these are not confused with living processes which are of an entirely different order; a confounding of the two orders would result in technological enslavement. Our task therefore is to continually emphasize the importance of engaging with questions of living intelligence and its ontology before we start to talk about an artificial or synthetic variety, which is a dead thing. It is the task of education to make the distinctions clear and put each in its proper place.

Such being the intent, let us see what we can gather from the foregoing lines that are pedagogically helpful toward building a dialogic future. The first difference between the two ontologies—conscious intelligence and artificial intelligence—is the capacity for problematization, for which genius is necessary. Once a problem is set up, it is relatively easy to work toward a solution, and a variety of tools including AI can be pressed into service to seek it. Each problematization in modern science, including those of Ernst Mach, Niels Bohr, Wolfgang Pauli, Albert Einstein, Werner Heisenberg, Erwin Schrödinger, to name but a few, was a leap of faith into the Unknown, based on learned intuition and extrapolation. No machine intelligence can do this because all algorithms, no matter how sophisticated, come out of past ontologies; only the living can be truly emergent because it is led on by uncertain elicitations and creative sources that are not fully understood.

The second difference we find with regard to embodied intelligence is its aporetic relation with the frontiers of the known. What does that signify? The furious debate between scientists about the meaning of the strange behavior of photons/lightwaves as well as the trajectory of electrons is indicative of an aporetic disjunction. The fact that one version—the Schrodinger wave equation—eventually came to be the dominant version does not mitigate this fact. And what is the fact? It is that as each version or theory aims into the dark, their hitting something does not bring total clarity, but only raises more questions. This is very important to understand. AI goes from the known to the known, whereas at the frontiers of knowledge, organic intelligence goes from aporia to aporia, and occasionally produces firm knowledge as a dialectical spin-off.

The third difference of embodied intelligence lies in complementarity and simultaneous multi-level thinking. Organic, conscious intelligence has multiple avenues of proceeding—rational thought, intuitive intelligence, corporeal awareness, archetypal knowledge, and mythical beliefs among others. All or some of these can be activated at the same time to bring about a complex and complementary understanding. Machine intelligence is information or data based, and has no possibility of complementarity. Even its indeterminacy, where it exists, is of a single dimension or degree of freedom. Conscious intelligence, on the other hand, can check its intuitive understanding against reasoned thinking or vice versa, among other things, and not be bound by either. From a pedagogic point of view, it is very important to acknowledge this since we typically tend to underplay the intuitive angle in intellectual and scientific work. While reasoned thinking and first order logic are vitally important, we must equally find ways to enhance the other modes of perception that distinguishes conscious intelligence from the artificial.

The next level of difference may be called the authorial difference, or the difference authored by aesthetic preferences of grouping. In other words, in doing scientific work, one may be led by aesthetic preferences that may be explicit or subliminal. Principles such as Occam's razor, theoretical elegance, and thought economy are aesthetic choices that in turn lead to the selecting and grouping of variables in the formation of theories. Machines work according to pragmatics and not according to aesthetics. The "meta" level of understanding that includes aesthetics is available only to living intelligence simply because it is working from an aesthetics of culture and not from a mechanical base. And without aesthetics we truly are reduced to machines. It is this collapse to a lower ontological plane that is sought to be prevented.

What we have attempted here is to lay bare the immaturity of speaking about an artificial something when we have no real understanding of what the authentic original is. It is akin to invoking artificial love when we do not know what love is. The danger in such thoughtless discourse is that proper inquiry into the original is bypassed and replaced by the simulacrum, because the mechanical version can be toyed with and controlled by the name-givers and the technocrats in dominant positions within society. The evidence of living intelligence is the presence of an ethico-aesthetic dimension that is free of narcissism, in particular, technocratic narcissism, for that is easily coopted. In the conversations reported above, one can see the exchanges of deep conviction without narcissism or egotism. The search for the ground of reality leads the thinkers to the cosmic realm wherein references to divine providence or a transcendent Nature are neither unwarranted nor alien. Among many things, it implies that the source of human intelligence is not available to the products or expressions of intelligence howsoever these may be named. Nevertheless, nomenclatures can be confounding to the growing mind, and can divert attention away from what needs attention, and what needs specific pedagogic attention today is not the digitalized, corporatized, monetized, militarized, privatized, and therefore patronized, form of intelligence, but the one that is the emergent actualization of human potential, the one that allows us to seek out the authentic in ourselves. And there can be no artificial mimicking of this living quality, it being a journey that living intelligence must organize for itself such that it is always facing toward the authentic and the Open.

CHAPTER 4

Rhythms of the Sentient

In this chapter, we are going to examine whether the secular (non-esoteric) and empirical form of measurable intelligence is the only kind of intelligence worth taking into consideration when we speak about education. And whether there are other forms that remain submersed or ignored in the march to contemporaneity that need to be recognized. For it is arguable that the world of human problems, at levels other than the purely logical or the symbolic, may not be reducible or solvable in terms of truth functions or be framed entirely in symbolic terms from which convergent outputs (justified truths) useful for educating may be derived. Rather, these are sometimes grasped more in terms of diffused emanations, non-localizable, and even embodied sensibilities, that may be extremely important from an educational as well as existential point of view. In other words, there may be many more types of sub-systemic intelligences that help us make sense of our world and generate useful meanings than conventionally understood ones such as mathematical or linguistic abilities. These might include some of the more important aspects of existentials, such as the manner in which we arrive at our general feelings about life, what we choose to do in terms of a living or a vocation, who we choose as our life-partner, whether we choose to adhere to the straight path or the crooked one, what we expect from our governments and representatives, how or what we salvage from setbacks or misfortunes in life, whether we feel our circumstances to be antagonistic or favorable, the lessons we learn

K. Roy, *Education, "Artificial" Intelligence, and Cognition*,
https://doi.org/10.1007/978-3-031-82263-6_4

or choose not to learn from experience, the dilemmas we face and how we handle them, how we prepare to face the intimation of our own eventual passing away as well as the loss of significant others, and so on. These and many other real-life challenges bear very little relationship with what is conventionally taken to be intelligence. For instance, one's competency in mathematics says nothing about one's ability to be comfortable in relationships, or one's capacity to be a reasonable neighbor. One's knowledge of economics does not necessarily make one good at handling personal finances or being creditworthy. Extensive knowledge of science or poetics does not make one a scientist or a poet. Nevertheless, the above challenges are what, for the large part, decide the quality of life of the individual (his/her life sustaining capacity), and not some objective, convergent, easily quantifiable quotient. The lesson is that high IQ, a conventional measure of high intelligence, does not necessarily make a thoughtful citizen or a creative agent.

Admittedly, highly selective slicing of reality using objective apparatuses of convergent intelligence may lead to significant changes in material circumstances of life, but these may not alter the affective and moral conditions at the individual or collective level that are relevant for intelligent living. The qualitative determinants of the latter consisting of divergent pathways are sometimes grouped under the term experiential intelligence.

> Experiential Intelligence, or XQ for short, is the combination of mindsets, abilities, and know-how gained from your unique life experience that empowers you to achieve your goals, wherein,
>
> - Mindsets are your attitudes and beliefs about yourself, other people, and the world that influence your personal and professional success.
> - Abilities are your personal competencies that help you integrate all that you have gained from your experience so you can respond to situations in the most effective way possible.
> - Know-how is your knowledge and skills.
> - XQ is your unique internal fingerprint—no one else possesses your distinct combination of mindsets, abilities, and knowhow because no one else has lived your experience.[1]

For instance, in writing a book, I do not have access to any special data or knowledge beyond what is available to most reasonably educated individuals concerned with the particular domain. However, the book is a

[1] Soren Kaplan, *Experiential Intelligence*, (Dallas, TX: Matt Holt Books, 2023), pp. 27–28.

product of knowledge only in part. For the larger part, it is the wringing out of experience that reconstitutes knowledge, and makes visible what is known by means of a special affective intensity. This is the writer's "unique internal fingerprint." The affective experience is the "flesh" on the skeleton of knowledge that gets written out in language. I say "written out" advisedly, because language provides only a mold in which the individual affective experience is die-cast by intricate processes about which we only have limited understanding. But could all of these be accounted for by some narrow quantitative measurement of some abstraction? My considered answer is that I do not think so.

> Even with all the available models and measures, something's missing today that doesn't quite capture how our individual intricacies can, and do, contribute to both success and satisfaction in life. We need a way to understand how everything we've obtained from our unique life experiences—no matter how mundane or significant—holistically contributes to our ability to show up in the world and achieve our goals. We need a way to articulate and justify why we might want to hire someone who's not "officially" qualified for a job, but who we know will do a great job anyway. We need a way to recognize the inherent wisdom and strength that exist in all of us because of what we've done and experienced in both our personal and professional lives. And we need a way to make the process of understanding, appreciating, and leveraging the power of unique experiences and differences something that we embrace in our teams, organizations, communities, and personal lives.[2]

We construct the world simultaneously in unique as well as collective ways. There is an organic tension between the two that makes our entire cognitive apparatus dialectically move forward. At times the gap is large, for instance, when we are writing poetry or doing art, because here individual vision may be at some distance from societal perception. At other times, the gap may be almost non-existent, such as when we are doing mathematics, which consists of agreed-upon symbolic meanings and their universally accepted modes of manipulation. To put it differently, there seems to be, in any sensible-intelligible activity, a two-fold process that can be thought of as interactions between an individual "anode" and a collective "cathode," resulting in flashes between these two nodes that may result in a semantically cognizable output. Again, one end of it consists of

[2] Ibid., p. 14.

collective (dead) knowledge of the system, and the other end is brought up by living neuro-phenomenological changes in the organism or pathemata. In the frequent interactions between these two nodes, that completely redefine our understanding of subjective/objective distinctions, are born intelligible and meaningful arc-moments that require a new language of expression.

> We're starting to see organizations, academics, and the popular press recognize that there's a broader way to look at intelligence. We've understood for a while that we need to tap into the intellect to solve problems. We've also embraced the importance of tuning into emotions as an important tool for leading and working with other people. We're just now starting to fully appreciate that, to effectively operate in today's world and adapt to the fast-paced, disruptive changes happening all around us, we need to tap into a different dimension of our intelligence—the intelligence developed out of experience. … It's not just about the hard skills we may develop to do something; it's also about the way we think and the abilities we develop that become part of who we are as people.[3]

Let us explore the peculiarity of experiential intelligence with an example. I refer to my own experience of writing. To start with, the consciousness (mental plane) is filled with tidbits of disjointed images, rather like litter circling lazily in gentle wind. Once all that is swept aside, the affective energies begin to get centered and focused, eventually forming a unified beam. It is this unified beam (so long as it lasts) that goes to work and becomes the writing instrument. The self, or the me, is not of much use here, except in checking to see, from time to time, if the writing (emanations) is on track and aligned with original intentions (dead knowledge). Without this yoke of knowledge, the creative function may get carried away, eventually becoming a nuisance to the publisher as well as the reader. Thus, the ego is only a constraint on what gets written, and not substantially the author. So, who is the writer, as a matter of experience? It is a question I have often asked myself. I have never received an adequate or satisfactory answer. But as a matter of experience what appears to be the case (in my case, that is), is that to begin with there is an in-gathering or raised intensity somewhere at the back of the throat, an intensifying movement that somehow connects to the network of neural and mento-emotional energies above it, and one begins to receive a gentle seepage, a

[3] Ibid., p. 15.

trickle of something that takes the formal shape of expression. The starting point is the in-gathering of affect that begins to get concentrated at a region and rises to the plane of representation. Now, I have attempted to present the experience in a raw form, without trying to mediate by complicated explanations. But if pressed, I would like to call it an organocentric manner of expression, wherein the whole organism is pressed into action in order to supersede the ego and regain stream-of-consciousness. However, the point here is that this description is so different than the usual manner of talking about writing that this could be thought of as a kind of uniqueness, while at the same time it cannot be denied that some form of intelligence is involved. Putting the two together we arrive at a diverse picture of intelligence, more diverse than most contemporary thinking would like to imagine or admit, due to the fact that there is a strong predilection for convergence. Sudden expansions or modifications in consciousness in which the usual dualities are left behind are neither understood nor acknowledged. Besides, in these modified mental landscapes not dominated by the symbol, a built-in species exceptionalism central to convergence is challenged. In other words, secular humanism is set aside and a cosmic organism is experienced.

> [Modernistic] ecology is predicated upon an assumption of manifest species exceptionalism. The entangled mess of experience is thus categorically sundered into two mutually exclusive objects, whereby an intrinsically human order of knowledge and reason, agency and subjectivity, appears to be self-evidently distinct from a non-human order of "nature," from a mere "environment" of inert "resources," subject-less "processes," and enclosable "property." And with this act of cosmic dichotomy, moderns have also sundered their world forever from most if not all non-modern worlds. They have irrevocably distanced themselves from peoples whose modes of being were governed by the unchanging annual rhythms of the seasons and the heavenly bodies, by the life cycles of animals and plants, from peoples who knew the lands that nurtured them in some sense as their parents or ancestors, from peoples who took it for granted that countless non-human agents and subjects were always out there, immanent in earth, sky, rivers, and seas, making all human life possible.[4]

[4] Greg Anderson, "Retrieving the Lost Worlds of the Past: The Case for an Ontological Turn," *The American Historical Review, Volume 120, Issue 3, June 2015*, Pages 787–810, https://doi.org/10.1093/ahr/120.3.787.

The so-called human order of (convergent) intelligence, based on assessments associated with superficial or surface level activity covering the surface of the earth and neighboring space, is of a self-serving kind. There is no objective or independent basis for deciding the intrinsic worth or quality of such activity, that is, whether it is of a liberating or destructive order. The usual justification is by claiming species exceptionalism, wherein the human order is assumed to be somehow different and more intelligent than the surrounding natural forces which are seen as "blind" and unintelligent. This "cosmic dichotomy" has led to fundamental discontinuities between the world and ourselves, leading one to doubt the veracity of an intelligence that often seems rather unintelligent when measured in terms of planetary consequences. It would suffice to take a couple of examples to illustrate the point. Let us consider two kinds of accumulation or enclosures, the first of wealth and the second of knowledge. Without belaboring the point, it is arguable that neither has added to planetary or even species well-being beyond a point. And yet vast energies are directed at these endeavors that act as proxies for well-being at individual and societal levels. As we proceed in time toward modernity as an age, intelligence is progressively reduced from a cosmic-level understanding to the level of the individual, and has further made possible notions such as machinic intelligence.

> This ontological individualism would have been scarcely intelligible to, say, the inhabitants of precolonial Bali or Hawai'i, where the divine king or chief, the visible incarnation of the god Lono, was "the condition of possibility of the community," and thus "encompasse[d] the people in his own person, as a projection of his own being," such that his subjects were all "particular instances of the chief's existence." It would have been barely imaginable, for that matter, in the world of medieval Europe, where conventional wisdom proverbially figured sovereign and subjects as the head and limbs of a single, primordial "body politic" or corpus mysticum. And the idea of a natural, presocial individual would be wholly confounding to, say, traditional Hindus and the Hagen people of Papua New Guinea, who objectify all persons as permeable, partible "dividuals" or "social microcosms," as provisional embodiments of all the actions, gifts, and accomplishments of others that have made their lives possible.[5]

[5] Ibid.

This could be a useful point to stray into some cross-cultural and non-contemporary views on intelligence such as the Indic. Basically, the Indic or ancient Indian view of intelligence revolved around the idea of *prajnya* or wisdom. A cognate notion is *jnana* which implies knowledge.[6] The relation between the two is best understood allegorically. Knowledge acts like a cleansing agent as well as an ordering principle putting things in their proper perspective and logical categories. After adequate preparation, wisdom (an ontological Otherness) enters to connect the being (microcosm) to the cosmic principle (macrocosm). This process in its entirety may be thought of as the operation of intelligence. Here intelligence rests neither in the individuality nor in the externality, but in an ongoing existential relation between the two, resulting in an intensification that takes the individual to more elevated orbits that are progressively free of fear and egotism. Intelligence is primarily this loss of fear and egotism due to the cosmic influence. Contrary to modernist views, intelligence here is not an addition but a loss—of false ideas and views. It may be understood as a kind of rarefication of consciousness resulting in higher receptivity and sensitivity to cosmic currents. There are no external measures for this kind of intelligence other than one's conduct in the world that is identified by displacement of self-centeredness by cosmic-centeredness.

But the measurable intelligence has served to harden the certainties about whose truths are more abiding, has come to be in charge of history and historicism, and has become thus a proxy for a truly comprehensive understanding of the human condition. In actuality, all that measurable intelligence can do, and has done, is to stretch the limits of its own boundaries. It cannot cross those boundaries and look at itself from the outside. In modernity, the non-secular or cosmic perspective has been discounted, resulting in the internalist perspective becoming the proxy for the whole, resulting in warped history.

> For more than a century now, the modernist certainties have been directly and indirectly challenged by influential currents of thought in a wide array of fields, from philosophy and critical theory to science studies and quantum physics. By drawing on the most powerful of these currents, we can in turn

[6] The Sanskrit words *prajnya* and *jnana* are difficult to articulate for the uninitiated. The first sounds more like "pra*ng*ya" and the second is close to "*ng*yana," with the "*ng*" as in the last syllable of "thi*ng*" in both cases. There are no English equivalents for these sounds.

> begin to formulate an alternative historicism, one that sees realness itself in an entirely new way: not as an objective, pre-given material condition but as a process, as an ongoing effect produced by the dynamic entanglement of thought and materiality. Hence, this heterodox form of historicism would require us to take an ontological turn in our practice. It would oblige us to make sense of each past lifeworld in its own metaphysical environment, because whatever our non-modern subjects collectively believed was always already there in their worlds would be an active, constitutive ingredient of whatever was really there at the time. And if we are prepared to make this move, we will duly produce histories that are at once more ethically defensible, more theoretically robust, and more historically meaningful.[7]

The above comments although written in the context of history are relevant here, for what is history but the record of human performance, and what is human performance but the history of the development of the thinking of the species. Combining the two we make the observation that there has been plenty of critical thinking on the subject, however, to date there has been no clear formulation of an alternative approach to the historical form of intelligence. The reason for that is not far to seek. The existing mode of thinking about human success and intelligence has served the ruling classes, especially the technocrats, well. And since the technocrat is the natural ally of the bureaucrat, it stands to reason that there has been no serious challenge to the paradigm at the ground level or at the level of social activity including education. As a result, what does the ordinary person associate with intelligence? It is unlikely to be in terms of how someone minimizes use of resources, or shows great consideration for others, but rather in terms of their knowledge of calculus or their control of social discourses, and so on. In other words, intelligence is considered not in terms of qualitative or aggregate social consequences but in terms of specialized skills, individualized competencies, or competitive advantage.

This epistemic of individualization, or methodological atomism is taken to a new level in the narratives that swirl around modern science. For example, we are often told in scientific discourse that at the sub-atomic level, the act of observation changes the reality, meaning that we can no longer be certain about all aspects of the behavior of the particle under observation, since particles are disturbed by the very force of the intervention. Now, what is obscured in the process of such claim making is that it is human intelligent activity that isolates and atomizes the particle in the

[7] Ibid.

first place. Next, the same intelligence claims that the observed phenomenon is disturbed by the observer at a sub-atomic level. All along, the lens is one of individualization and fragmentation, but when we learn to treat the world as patterns and ensembles, no such easy separation is possible. Thus the scientific loose talk is dismissed by none other than Werner Heisenberg himself, the father of the famed uncertainty principle.

> I find all such assertions as 'observation introduces uncertainty into the phenomenon' inaccurate and misleading. Nature has taught us that the word 'phenomenon' cannot be applied to atomic processes unless we also specify what experimental arrangement or what observational instruments are involved. If a particular experimental setup has been defined and a particular observation follows, then we can admittedly speak of a phenomenon, but not of its disturbance by observation. And though the results of different observations can no longer be correlated as directly as they could in classical physics, this does not mean that the phenomena have been disturbed by observation; it simply means that we cannot objectify the observational results in the manner of classical physics or everyday experience. Different observational situations—by that I mean the over-all experimental setup, the readings, etc.—are often complementary.[8]

In actuality, the uncertainty principle affirms the unbroken continuity of ontological reality. It implies that when we make a break in continuity, apparent bedevilments occur, since the complementary nature of things resist one-sided measurements. A similar thing happens in thinking of intelligence. In the assessment of the ensemble "+individual+context+stim ulus+observer+," one can never be certain whether a measurement reflects more of the physical context, the changing pathemata, the response to stimuli, or the inherent bias of the measurement, because all of it together form a multi-sided gestalt. We can even say that intelligence is better thought of as complementary emanations of multiple blessings rather than as isolated concentrations attributable to a subject. The greater the intensity or demand in a situation, the more adequate might be the response; on the other hand, an anemic or depleted context might result in an uninvolved or equivocal response in the ensemble. Thus what we get through conventional measurements is a proxy element that stands in for actuality, for that actuality is not really quantifiable or measurable as such.

[8] Werner Heisenberg, *Physics and Beyond* (New York: Harper & Row, 1971), p. 105.

At this point I wish to take us deeper into the question of proxy intelligence as distinguishable from the phenomenological arc-moments of the ensemble that I mentioned earlier—a distinction of the fake from the real. I shall do so by means of a reference to John Searle's work and his famous Chinese Room Argument (CRA). Here, Searle argues that it is possible to carry out syntactical manipulations that give the *impression* of semantical grounding, but it does not amount to actual understanding. A more commonplace analogy might be the parroting of words by bird or beast without comprehension. Many animals can ape human language to a surprising degree of perfection, but of course it does not mean that they understand the ontic references or cultural meanings inherent in the sounds they are mouthing.

> Searle argues that understanding, of say a Chinese story, can never arise purely as a result of following the procedures prescribed by any computer program; for Searle offers a first-person tale outlining how he could instantiate such a program, and act as the Central Processing Unit of a computer, produce correct internal and external state transitions, pass a Turing test for understanding Chinese, and yet still not understand a word of Chinese. Searle describes a situation whereby he is locked in a room and presented with a large batch of papers covered with Chinese writing that he does not understand. Indeed, the monoglot Searle does not even recognise the symbols as being Chinese, as distinct from say Japanese or simply meaningless patterns. Later Searle is given a second batch of Chinese symbols, together with a set of rules (in English) that describe an effective method (algorithm) for correlating the second batch with the first, purely by their form or shape. Finally he is given a third batch of Chinese symbols together with another set of rules (in English) to enable him to correlate the third batch with the first two, and these rules instruct him how to return certain sets of shapes (Chinese symbols) in response to certain symbols given in the third batch.[9]

A level of accuracy in the following of syntactical procedures can be achieved that passes a Turing test, meaning it is comparable in achievement to a human level of competency, but this is not an indication of an understanding of the reality behind the linguistic signifiers. By means of the CRA thought experiment, Searle shows that even without any semantic understanding of the referents, it is possible to maintain increasingly

[9] Vincent C. Muller (Ed.), *Philosophy and Theory of Artificial Intelligence* (New York: Springer, 2013), p. 24.

sophisticated sets of correlations that can pass a Turing test. A simple analogy that might be familiar to teachers everywhere is that students can mimic learning by reproducing memorized or selectively guided responses in assessments without much understanding of the subject matter. But getting back to CRA,

> The central claim of the CRA is that computations alone cannot in principle give rise to understanding, and that therefore computational theories of mind cannot fully explain human cognition. More formally, Searle stated that the CRA was an attempt to prove that syntax (rules for the correct formation of sentences: programs) is not sufficient for semantics (understanding). Combining this claim with those that programs are formal (syntactical), whereas minds have semantics, led Searle to conclude that 'programs are not minds'. And yet it is clear that Searle believes that there is no barrier in principle to the notion that a machine can think and understand; indeed in MBP Searle explicitly states, in answer to the question 'Can a machine think?', that 'the answer is, obviously, yes. We are precisely such machines'. Clearly Searle did not intend the CRA to target machine intelligence per se, but rather any form of artificial intelligence according to which a machine could have genuine mental states (e.g. understanding Chinese) purely in virtue of executing an appropriate series of computations: what Searle termed 'Strong AI'.[10]

From the above discussion it is clear that formal syntactical capabilities as such do not equate to mind, and so the computational model of the mind and of human intelligence is rejected. But as to the question, can a machine think, Searle is in the affirmative, and goes so far as to say, humans are thinking machines. And here, I beg to differ, for I do not believe that Searle has sufficiently gone into the question of what it means to think. One person who has done so is Martin Heidegger, and I shall make a reference here to his position on this aspect in *Being and Time*. From the Heideggerian point of view, in the simplicity and directness of being there is nothing to think, for there is no supplementary dimension other than the fullness of being. It is in the withdrawal from being that thinking begins. The machine is a child of this thinking that arises from a divorce—the divorce from self-nature or being. Hence, in saying that we are thinking machines, Searle is looking at the phenomenon of thinking from the wrong end of the scope. The machine and machinic intelligence can do

[10] Ibid.

marvelous things, but it can never be authentic, meaning to be the true author of its own actions. Its source is always a programming, and besides, it cannot refuse that programming. Therein lies a fundamental difference between human intelligence and machinic ones.[11]

> The post-Turing scientific endeavors have all struggled with the possibility of equating human intelligence with machines or robots, insisting that machines could actually be programmed in certain ways to act and think intelligently like humans. The question then arises, what does it mean to be intelligent? And what mechanism is needed to produce it? Heidegger's idea of intelligence as "being", flows from his [idea of] authenticity as a true dasein. Heidegger argues that whatever we think, and the decisions we make, are products of our authenticity as humans rather than mechanical computability. Machines, irrespective of their applaudable skills and ground-breaking displays, follow the rules of man's dominance within the context of tools and goals. They are so by nature and their being cannot be fulfilled, unlike man, whose nature is herculean with complexities that go beyond algorithmic and computational manipulations.[12]

To equate authenticity or being with intelligence is a good way to start making a proper distinction between living intelligence and mechanistic ones. Authentic comes from the Greek "auto" meaning self or selfsame. And when in turn we pose the question as to the source of the self, there is a thickly silence, for who can know the source of the self—one has to be logically beyond and prior to the self to know its source, which is impossible. This impossibility is the ground for a spontaneous ignition; in other words, the self bursts upon the scene, totally unlike a machine which needs the stoking of algorithms and programs primarily designed by human hands. That is to say, the so-called machine intelligence is a simulated product and not an autonomous or authentic one that is the life of being. The being of the machine on the other hand is inauthentic, a copy. This is important to establish once and for all, otherwise we remain mired in a dangerous confusion and continue to romance foolish notions, thus reducing the potential becoming of the human.

[11] A human being can go against the life instinct and spontaneously commit suicide, but the machine can self-destruct only if at some point instructed to do so via an algorithm.

[12] Ogonyi Francis Ekaya, "Heideggerian Critique Of Artificial Intelligence: Where Machines Have Failed In The Human-Robots Comparism" *Journal of Rare Ideas, Vol. 2. Nos. 2, September, 2021*, p. 47.

> Heidegger makes the case beginning with his concept of authentic and inauthentic existence. Robots as argued here are inauthentic designs whose being cannot be achieved. To exist authentically, a being should be able to acknowledge the groundlessness of human existence, acting resolutely and shaping its world as well as defining it (Heidegger, 520). Man at this level, assumes the seat as the principal subject of his actions, where he decides for himself rather than being decided for. This subjectivity, could be likened to the subjective analysis of Descartes in his cogito ergo sum. Descartes, expanded on the idea of the "self" as the "I" who thinks, judges, decides, argues and acts from his subjective consciousness. This consciousness, which for him emanates from consciously active being, who thinks for himself rather than being assembled and controlled. His analysis of intelligence was anti-physicist, as evident in his statement "brute cannot think, equivalent as machines cannot think" (Descartes quoted in Nath, 30). The subjective self of Descartes is one whose consciousness allows him take actions which are said to be intelligent. Away from that, he is no different from a brute, or said to be an inauthentic agent. Inauthentic existence on the other hand, is to be lost in the conformism of the crowd. It is a situation where one cannot even discover himself or take responsibility for his own existence, but rather lost where he relies on the directives of laid down rules.[13]

The most important notion to be noted above is the reference to the "groundlessness of human existence." It is a reference to the appearance of the sense of intelligent being from nothingness or unknowingness. All machines appear from a previous line or ground of development, whereas human consciousness is not grounded in anything, not even in a prior animal consciousness. All reference to the source or ground of human consciousness will therefore always be purely speculative and even nonsensical, for the very notion of source or ground itself is an invention within consciousness. In other words, using words as self-descriptors is futile precisely because those very expressions are the concoctions of the self. Self-referentiality as a point of reference for comparison with machinic ontology is poor metaphysics indeed. Thus it is that,

> AI for Heidegger is a project in crisis due to its immaturity. He posits: "the search for the capacity to model human intelligence is so huge that we are far from the comfort zone of knowing how to ask the right question" (502). The more we attempt to understand what the science of AI is trying to put forward, the more we are confused. Lamenting further, he observed that "If

[13] Ibid., p. 51.

> we gather a body of science and use it without challenging it, then we will not be doing science anymore." … Heidegger faults the science of Artificial Intelligence for equating man with machines without first digging into the complexities surrounding the being of man.[14]

In common parlance, artificial means a synthetic copy of some natural substance, phenomenon, or activity, including an artificial smile or synthetic vinegar. What is beyond doubt is that the reference point of the artificial is the natural or the organic. Hence, when we use the signifier artificial intelligence, the implied signification is that it is a copy or simulation or approximation of natural intelligence. But the point is that till date we know next to nothing about the nature, root, or phenomenology of natural intelligence. What we have is a lot of learned guesswork, disputed theories, but no real answers. Leave alone finding answers, we do not even know what the right questions might be when it comes to understanding human intelligence. We can ape different aspects of it, but as we understand neither the process nor its source, all attempts to copy human intelligence in machines are bound to be limited and severely restricted. We must be humble enough to acknowledge this fact; otherwise, we only succeed in spreading confusion. For machines are never autonomic, nor are they "capable of disobeying what they have been programmed to do. One cannot gain knowledge of the world or reality in this kind of situation. It is in this category that robots or machines find themselves. Ontological inauthenticity is a big vacuum in their existence."[15] Machines have no being-in-the-world, that is, awareness of a complex world out there, other than the immediate measurements their instruments have been set up to record. Their ontological inauthenticity is instantiated by the example that a machine sent to Mars does not understand why it is on Mars, even as it carries out intelligent programs on the Martian landscape, nor does it care about its return to the earth.

> The arguments show that intelligent behavior is closely knitted in one's conscious ability. A thing must be conscious before it can be said to exercise intelligent behaviors otherwise we only rest on mere assumption and speculation that robots actually are intelligent. Conscious activity proceeds from the human brain, and how the brain works to produce this conscious activity is still a mystery. The activities of the brain are complex and still far from

[14] Ibid., p. 50.
[15] Ibid.

> human comprehension. Buttressing this point, Epstein remarks: We may assume that the brain works like a computer, its processing could work by analogy with computational processes. It is also true that it is a physical entity like computers, and works with signals, resolves complex problems. Nevertheless, the way the brain works is still unknown, and it may not be a digital computation or information processing computation where inputs are changed to outputs (Epstein, https://aeon.co/essays). In reaction to this, Martinez-Miranda and Aldea, are of the opinion that "it is impossible to imagine that some properties of being alive could be replicated without the distinctive properties of being alive. Therefore machines do not have autonomy nor do they reproduce like humans do" (Emotions in Human and Artificial Intelligence, 15). Simply put, only the human brain is capable of conscious activity, it is not possible to duplicate the brain and have it work well. Machines are unconscious material things, while humans are both conscious and material. The human brain that produce conscious activity, only stops working when one dies, a situation that automatically brings consciousness to an automatic halt.[16]

But what does it mean to be conscious? This question would not arise if I were alone in the world without a second ontic item. Consciousness is neither data processing nor algorithmic computation, for it is prior to information. When the growing fetus in the womb smiles or kicks, it is in a pre-informational state. Its whole being is directly responding to the maternal conditions without mediation. In part, this direct response to the world and our being-in-the-world unmediated by calculation is living consciousness. Pure consciousness has no content or intent. Contra Husserl, it simply is. On the contrary, the machine has no spontaneous is-ness. It is started by algorithm, maintained by algorithm, modified by algorithm, and shut down by algorithm. While the human brain-mind may, in some respects, appear analogous to computers, such appearance by no means establishes that it is in fact operating as such. The backward engineering does not reveal even for a moment the true mystery of living consciousness. No one in the world has a clue as to how the living consciousness grapples with complex situations or organizes them or even has the idea of making a computer to speed up routine processing. My claim here is that living consciousness is *not an apparatus*, whereas a machine, however sophisticated, is an apparatus, a deliberate contraption built for a purpose. And while it can simulate certain reasoning processes, it has no

[16] Ibid., p. 53.

being-in-the-world even remotely parallel to the living being. Such being the case, and human intelligence being an offshoot of living consciousness, the latter is categorically different than machine intelligence, and it is utterly unfruitful to bring the two into comparison.

> Heidegger wraps up this case [by] approaching consciousness from the angle of dasein as a being-unto-death. He argues that as a being on to death, man expresses his consciousness towards his finitude. That is to say that, it is only a being that is conscious that thinks about his impending end, where he gets engulfed in anguish, anxiety and fear, knowing that he lives today, tomorrow he dies. This awareness braces him up to live uprightly and exhaust his time in life, for it is only the living (who is conscious) that thinks about death. The words of Randell J and Buchleri, make sense in this regards: "death only makes meaning to a being that is conscious, transcendence is fundamental to a conscious being for whatever is known, is known only to the conscious being, and in consciousness alone are evidence weighed and its force determined" (57). We then reiterate our question, where do robots fit in, in the area of consciousness?[17]

Going deeper in an ontological direction we find that conscious intelligence is buffeted by the world of experience, making it aware of its finitude. This finitude becomes the center of its focus as it negotiates its position in the world. Humans build a society around this conundrum of a finite sojourn, struggling with this relentless fact, trying to hide from it, resisting it, and finally yielding to it. Death is only for the living; machinic intelligence is not a reaction to finitude as it has no death to think about. It is dead from the beginning. Death or finitude is written into living consciousness, and it makes it special. The challenge is to make the brief cameo meaningful.

Once there is clarity about the ontological difference, there is clarity about the need to differentiate organic or conscious intelligence from material or machinic ones, and put an end to loose, immature talk. Education must begin with this clarity. Rejecting machinic time, the living intelligence must learn to work in the opposite direction, that is with the fact of finitude. Its anxiety and desire for transcending finitude must be directed at the discovery of an eternal now independent of time. The first educational lesson therefore is that living intelligence must not use time as a bank account. It must learn to reject fake temporality and deny any

[17] Ibid., p. 54.

significance to finitude or indefinitude. It must believe in duration as distinct from time. This means, while futurism as a social attitude cannot be avoided, we must educate ourselves to live simultaneously on another plane in which the progression of events is seen as nothing but a circus—going around in circles—that has no lasting significance. Therefore, the timeless now is all that we have, and that must be lived fully. The intelligence of the timeless now or of simply being is of no use to the machine, but is of the greatest significance to the sentient. This obviously requires a lot of mature thinking and experimenting, but nevertheless needs to be articulated properly as a part of educational phenomenology.

The second educational lesson is to stop taking the babble around the Turing test narrative seriously. The comparison between machine intelligence and human intelligence is based on unutterable ontological confusion and perhaps even a degree of motivated social engineering. As Heidegger has pointed out, to talk of artificial intelligence before there is proper understanding of organic intelligence is to be disoriented and immature. We really have no proper understanding of what or how our consciousness perceives and does things—we only have the end products in view. We may assume that the brain works like a computer which is its own brain-child. But whether the material off-spring is anything like the living original is something about which no one has a clue. What is more, there is no known way to figure out what is going on in the brain simply because logically one would need a superior mind-brain to do that. Hence, putting electrodes in the brain won't do, cutting open dead brains won't do, scanning the structure won't do, because in each case, the part story cannot tell us about how the whole actually works. A proper recognition of this fact is not an admission of defeat but an acknowledgment of what is tenable.

The third educational lesson is that there is no hierarchy between machine intelligence and the human, simply because they belong to different ontological categories. Unlike the comparison between a baboon and a chimpanzee, or a rat and a mongoose, both of which pairs are living-organic ones, the comparison between human and machine is a meaningless exercise, no matter who wins in a chess game or a military exercise. A segmented activity with carefully constructed rules will not reveal any of the underlying fundamentals of general intelligence, and we have got to be seriously fooling ourselves if we believe it does. Some of us may find this denial difficult to stomach, nevertheless it is true that consciousness-related intelligence is groundless, meaning it has no known source save itself, whereas material intelligence is grounded in its makers, and this makes them fundamentally different and therefore noncomparable.

The next educational lesson to be drawn from this discussion is that machine intelligence is geared toward finding answers, whereas organic or living intelligence can pose the question. Important advances in knowledge come from the capacity to problematize and pose the right questions. It is in posing questions that authentic creativity lies. Once the question is posed there may be many ways of finding solutions, including computational or algorithmic ones. But the question comes first; the problem must be constructed before a solution is found. An authentic problem surfaces through being-in-the-world, and since machines have no being-in-the-world, they cannot generate authentic problems. In *Crime and Punishment* Dostoevsky poses the question about alienation and the nature of guilt. No machinic intelligence can do that for it has no experience of inner or ethical conflict, no matter how cleverly it is programmed to produce text. Likewise, Beethoven's Fifth Symphony is a question placed before the spirit, about its confrontation with fate. The composition is described by the famed music critic E.T.A. Hoffmann thus: "How this wonderful composition climbs on and on, leads the listener imperiously forward into the spirit world of the infinite! … No doubt the whole rushes like an ingenious rhapsody past many a man, but the soul of each thoughtful listener is assuredly stirred, deeply and intimately, by a feeling that is none other than that unutterable portentous longing, and until the final chord—indeed, even in the moments that follow it—he will be powerless to step out of that wondrous quest."[18] Through his music, Beethoven sets up the finitude of man against his longing for the infinite. It is ridiculous to suppose that such a problem can occur to a machine, however well-programmed it might be to produce melodies. Likewise, in physics, once the structure of the atom became scientific commonplace, innumerable calculations proceeded therefrom, and continue to do so today with the help of mainframes and data processors connected to accelerators. But the initiating point is always an onto-phenomenological moment, the result of authentic being-in-the-world. If our attention is riveted only on

[18] E.T.A. Hoffman, "Beethovens Instrumental-Musik", *Zeitung für die elegante Welt* [de], nos. 245–247 (9, 10, and 11 December 1813): cols. 1953–1957, 1964–1967, and 1973–1975. Translated by Joseph M Hayse (Schenectady: Union College Press, 1996); ISBN 0-912756-28-4. The Fifth Symphony had a long development process, as Beethoven worked out the musical ideas for the work. The first "sketches" (rough drafts of melodies and other musical ideas) date from 1804.

solutions, it is a serious form of ignorance, for then we fail to understand the genius of problem creation. The authentic problem, whether artistic, musical, scientific, or mathematical, is always and forever a stirring in the soul, a transcendent moment that is beyond the ken of machines.

The next educational point needing to be grasped is that the respective goals of intelligence associated with living consciousness and the intelligence attributed to machine learning are radically different. How can we say this with confidence? It cannot escape notice that the extraordinary growth in human intelligence (of the conventional kind) has been accompanied by extraordinary growth in human stupidity and violence. It is not as if human society has become a peaceful and compassionate oasis due to the marvels of technology. Without laboring the point regarding which plenty has already been said by other commentators, we can say that this contrapuntal movement reveals something. It tells us that technological intelligence whether of the human kind or the machinic kind, is not necessarily emancipatory, even if it brings distinct physical advantages to certain human groups. The physical advantages and conveniences do not add up to real advances in well-being or qualitative existence. Given this fact, it is not a wild assertion to say that machinic and technological intelligence are mere curiosities on the landscape of existence whereas qualitative improvements lie elsewhere. It is not easy to say where that elsewhere lies or readily determine its coordinates. It is, in fact, the task of living intelligence to figure out this otherness, the qualitative aspect of being in the world.

Educators are often asked about the role of AI in education, and this constitutes the last point in this discussion. I wish to categorically state that AI has no special role in education, apart from the fact that students must learn about machine intelligence just like any other subject matter or emergent topic of interest. What is meant by the above statement is that AI cannot have any active or meta role in education beyond being a subject of study. Learning algorithms, digital processing, and material transformations including cybernetic systems have an increasingly important role to play in social and technological management. Nevertheless, the human observer cannot be interpellated in these ongoing transformations, and must remain transcendent, simply because the human psyche is a non-temporal phenomenon. Psychiatrists and psychoanalysts have long known that there is no time element in the psyche. That is to say, it does not progress with time. The archetypes that dominate the interior landscape of the mind belong to culture that predates any individual and predates thinking itself. We have very little understanding as to how the collective consciousness operates beyond knowing that it somehow does. Perhaps one task of education is to further the depth of self-knowledge that might be afforded by such inquiry.

In summarizing the argument, I am at pains to point out that machine intelligence must not be seen in terms of successive approximations of the organic or living intelligence. It is not a comparative or competitive copy of the original but only a mimicking of certain limited syntactic expressions. It is a dangerous form of unethical romanticization that constructs and creates the irresponsible and misplaced belief in a proxy. Without taking away anything from machine capabilities, to draw any comparison between two entirely unlike categories is to spread misapprehensions about both. It also blunts the potential becoming of the organic by raising the bogey of the mechanical. The project of dumbing down of education is greatly facilitated by mixing up the two categories, whether deliberate or otherwise. Organic intelligence works innately toward liberation and emancipation, whereas mechanical intelligence is directed at efficiency and optimization. Thus the goals of the two are qualitatively different and may even be complementary, but the one cannot stand in for the other. Students must be educated to understand this fundamental difference; otherwise, one becomes deluded and irresponsible. At all times, the being of the human stands in a unique but differential relation to the technological, and it is part of education to discover what this relation is. Equally, the respect for the organic being is neither automatic nor can it be taken for granted; it must be cultivated and awakened. The respect for the being is not egoism nor self-respect, but is an attitude of ontological thankfulness, a graciousness that is expressed toward the cosmos without which we are reduced to a robotic (slave) society.

CHAPTER 5

The Mental and the Elemental

Interlocutor:	Till now you have remained reticent about what intelligence actually is according to you, preferring to address the issue indirectly, even vicariously.
Author:	In any meaningful inquiry, some of the existing baggage surrounding the terms in question have to be examined first. No? We cannot afford to be too quick to arrive at definitions, otherwise the inquiry is foreclosed.
I:	But surely we have to be, at least incrementally, clear about the terms?
A:	No doubt clarity has to be achieved eventually, but not in haste. We do not know if there is anything universal like intelligence in the first place, and whether it is not a fabrication of the human mind belonging to territorially advantaged groups looking into a hall of mirrors.
I:	How else can we debate the matter?
A:	We are not debating, but inquiring. The writer did not begin this exercise by knowing what intelligence is or is not and then settled down to write about it. I am as much a part of the inquiry as my readers, and I am frankly surprised by what is gradually unfolding as we go deeper into the question.

K. Roy, *Education, "Artificial" Intelligence, and Cognition*,
https://doi.org/10.1007/978-3-031-82263-6_5

I: Then it seems what you are saying is that intelligence is non-localizable, and we have to proceed simultaneously on many fronts somewhat like an atmospheric phenomenon, thus side-stepping the need for a definition which forces us to become localized.

A: It is not possible to categorically state, at least at this point, whether the phenomenon we have been referring to as intelligence is an open or a closed system, if that's your implication.

I: It is not clear to me what you mean, open or closed with respect to what?

A: Is intelligence a "system" in respect of the human being with definable parameters such as the rules of first order logic? If it is, then it must have a closure of some kind, in the sense of a system/environment separation. Or is intelligence a continual becoming of patterns, connections, meanings, sustenances, concentrations, and openings that are fundamentally unbounded, in other words, an outpouring of potentialities?

I: Why is that relevant at this point?

A: If intelligence, assuming such a thing exists, is systemic then it can only expand within the system, somewhat like an expanding balloon. Then no matter how much it expands, it is still limited by its ontogenesis.

I: And if it is not systemic then what happens?

A: Then, it is not bounded by ordinary logic; it is transcendent, at least in *potentia*, which is the 'Open,' or what some refer to as God, or Nature, if you prefer.

I: That is too big a leap for me.

A: Don't apply the imagination. Stick to the sensibleness of the thing—limited or open.

I: You are arriving at God logically? No one has ever been able to do that.

A: That is because God or Nature is the obverse side of logic. I am merely alluding to it. You cannot see it from the side of logic, but it is nevertheless the condition of its possibility.

I: Makes it kind of essentialist, doesn't it? In that manner, each step we take must be dogged by God.

A: Of course. That is what the seers and mystics have always insisted.

I: This is becoming too thick for my taste.

A: So, let us get back on track. The question raised was about the hitherto inadequate formulation of the concept of intelligence in the present work.

I: Your point being that it is out of necessity of sorts.

A: You see, what makes the thing so difficult is that we are so good at duping ourselves. The name-givers invent a word, and in due course it attains ontological status. We can no longer doubt its existence.

I: If everyone agrees that there is such a thing, then what is the difficulty in accepting it as a valid representation of something actual?

A: There was a time when everyone believed that the earth was at the center of the world. We can think what we like, making things up as we go.

I: Most average people don't care one way or another. Their lives are not improved by changing the assumptions about the solar system.

A: Things are a little different in the present case however. Assumptions about intelligence have a profound effect on the social order.

I: How so?

A: Remember the famous line about ruling ideas being those of the ruling classes? Once established, we become accustomed to firm categories, but life cannot be put into categories, it is fluid, changing its contour from moment to moment.

I: But social life is not possible without categories—who is a citizen and who is not, what is a crime and what is not, where there is a contradiction and where there is none, and so on.

A: Perhaps that is true, but nevertheless functional categories must not be mistaken for ontological ones. Intelligence is at times treated as functional, and at other times as ontological.

I: And it is neither or both?

A: The trouble is, in asking that question you are using the mental faculty, and not some independent mechanism. In other words, you are using a part of the mind to judge an aspect or assumed characteristic of the mind itself. That is where the trouble starts, but it does not end there.

I: But surely we do that all the time, including when we judge a piece of art?

A: Art is not a product of the mind, although the mind may participate in its expression. Art is not art if we are not *moved* by it, thus showing the affective-impulsive side, but logic remains logic, whether you are affected or not.

I: So, we have to decide whether intelligence is on the side of logic or art?

A: In a way, yes. But that is only a part of the problem. It is not easy, however, to categorize an elusive phenomenon.

I: So, where do we go from here?

A: We have to generate a standpoint for observation that is not usually regarded as part of intelligence. We cannot articulate intelligence from within intelligence.

I: What could that alternate ground possibly be?

A: It obviously has to be from the aesthetic side. Love, goodwill, potential for being, or something of that order which is not from the empirical side of things.

I: Surely you do not mean personal or romantic love?

A: No. It is more like what the Buddhists and the Indians call *pragya* (or *prajnya*), that is, a form of wisdom-love, not unlike *agape* of the early Christians. A becoming-response of absoluteness from within that somatically connects all that was hitherto seemingly unconnected. This deeper connectedness provides a different perspective on things. It also permits another way of evaluating relations between things.

I: That is perhaps a useful manner of laying the ground for independent assessment—by means of connective relations.

A: Connective relations can usefully provide a contrast to the fragmentary relations that make up conventional intelligence.

I: Maybe you should clarify that a little bit. Why is conventional intelligence fragmentary?

A: The conventional approach in the discourse of intelligence is linked to some measurable outcome in the world wherein the measured subject is discrete and not continuous with the measurer. Moreover, if you are able to detect or make sense of an observable and I am not, you are deemed more intelligent than I. At the collective level, as societies get more sophisticated in terms of instrumentation or data processing or speed or something else, these are taken to be highly significant for competitive progress. There is a presumption of discreteness.

I: What are you suggesting instead?

A: This approach is obviously not going to change. But if you are going to question or inquire into "intelligence" then you have to seek a ground that is untainted by the presumed hierarchy which is innate to conventional intelligence.

I: And the organic interconnectedness of all phenomena is one such ground?

A: But it is easier said than done, the attainment of interconnectedness, that is. The human brain is not used to seeing in terms of interconnectedness. We need a sea change in perspective and to reeducate the whole being.

I: How can we do that?

A: It is not achieved in terms of information or knowledge, but in terms of practice. We have to change certain practices. Words are insufficient.

I: Where do we begin then?

A: Well, the first thing we need to do is to reconnect the spinal energies with the cerebral ones.

I: Surely you are kidding. The spine is already connected to the brain, if you mean that literally.

A: Yes, but only technically and minimally, so as not to be paraplegic. Proprioceptive, that's about it.

I: But somewhere you are suggesting that we *are* paraplegic in terms of the level and quality of our existential freedom and energy?

A: Just look around you and you will see the average quality of life. At this point in civilization, we are in a state of dissociated and assisted living—dissociated from ourselves, and assisted by devices, drugs, data processors, and so on. The entire civilization is on crutches, and we call the sum of these dependencies intelligent living, or species evolution, or something fancier.

I: What about all the celebrated feats of intelligence like trips to outer space, particle accelerators, chess-playing machines, quantum computing, and suchlike?

A: Which of these has enhanced how you feel about tomorrow or truly enriched your relationship to reality?

I: Probably none, not for me at least. The existential uncertainties have continued to gather like a dark cloud despite everything.

A: So our anxieties are not very different from those of the previous generations?

I: I think we can reasonably say that, perhaps even more than earlier. Nevertheless, what are these developments if not intelligent evolution or the evolution of intelligence?

A: Let us not jump the gun, as the saying goes, and make any claims. We will proceed with what's on hand. And what's experientially true is that while we have become incredibly sophisticated technologically as a species, our real problems in terms of collective suffering and existential disharmony have not diminished. Average distress like per capita social debt has only grown.

I: I do not think anyone can dispute that. There are enough indices available to support that assertion. But there is always hope.

A: We should not follow the false prophets. Hope is never in the future but in the living present.

I: Are you suggesting that intelligence as an operational characteristic is a false prophet, as it were?

A: I do not wish to characterize an unknown variable as this or that. That would be prejudicial to the inquiry. But the artificial thing is a false prophet by definition, because the very dictionary meaning of artificial is fake or inauthentic. So I am not saying anything about it for the moment.

Rather, I want to unearth the conditions that make us speak of such a thing in the first place. Each concept is the consequence of a prevailing set of conditions and circumstances.

I: These conditions and circumstances, are they accidental?

A: Nothing is accidental in this world. They appear to us as such because we are enabled to see only a part of the reality. The connections and links are occluded.

I: If we accept that for the moment, what are the conditions that have given rise to the discourse of intelligence?

A: Ideas of racial superiority, colonialism, militarism, these are some of the early precursors, the *pudenda origo* so to speak, to borrow a phrase from Nietzsche.

I: Lowly origins, eh?

A: Most glorified notions have dubious genealogy. It's almost a rule. Like we mentioned earlier, Marx used to say that all ruling ideas come from the ruling classes. And the ruling classes … we know where *they* come from.

I: Self-serving, in other words.

A: Quite so.

I: Coming back to the problem of generating an alternative ground for observing this attribute called intelligence, you suggested that we link two forms of energy, the spinal and the cerebral, or the somatic and the mento-emotional, to create a force field that is more holistic than intelligence. Would that be accurate?

A: It is from that "field" which is not the attribute of any individual or group that we can begin to understand the question of intelligence.

I: But the question remains, how is such a field possible?

A: The Native Americans often spoke of a field of force that permeated the entire tribe and extended to the natural world including the buffalo and the coyote.

I: Are you suggesting that such a field is always already there, and we have to become aware of it once more?

A: The unified field theory in science was a failed idea because the scientist could not include himself in it. S/he remained outside the field as an observer. But a true field is all-inclusive, immanent, and cannot leave the observer outside of itself.

I: And we can overcome this failing by linking the spinal with the mental, or the psychic with the cosmic?

A: All such linking is world-participation and requires a lot of work.

I: What kind of work?

A: Awaking the spinal energies is not an easy task. It is through the spine that we reach the world, and not through the mind.

I: Why are you prioritizing the spine?

A: Because the spinal column is the channel of the universal source; it is our link to the cosmos.

I: This is getting too esoteric, is it not?

A: We are constituted of the mental as well as the elemental. The elemental connection is preserved in the spine and the mental in the brain. Somehow, evolution has edged us closer to the brain to the neglect of the elemental. You can think of it as the body/mind split.

I: But what is wrong in thinking of intelligence as a mental capacity?

A: Nothing, nothing whatsoever. The problem is with accepting a dominant and unified definition of intelligence, not to speak of the artificial variety.

I: Intelligence has the odor of superiority; it has social power, is that the problem?

A: It bespeaks of rank ordering, which is problematic in a world of essential heterogeneity. But that is only part of the problem. The other part is what it invisibilizes or subsumes.

I: Back there you referred to practices. Can we go into it? It seems practices can break the deadlock of accepting intelligence as a transcendental signified.

A: The ancients spoke consistently of two things but in different ways. One is rhythm. Its roots in Vedic Sanskrit allude to an orderly flow.

I: What has rhythm got to do with this?

A: Well, you wouldn't have a world without rhythm. Matter emerges out of rhythm, out of patterned or synchronized vibrations. Layers and layers of waves in sync, or bound in phase, produce cosmic particles, and in turn, compound bodies like us. We have to keep this wave-like nature in mind as we proceed.

I: I am a little baffled by your sudden change of direction, but please go on.

A: I am trying to get to an alternative perch from where to understand the psycho-somatic link. Think of carnal pleasure and why we seek orgasm as a culmination. It is because it brings us closest to rhythm from our usual crystallized state. Deep conviviality produces erotic convulsions awaking primal being that is independent of civilization.

I: Freud said civilization is repressed Eros.

A: He was more right than he perhaps knew or could acknowledge. When societies begin to crystallize, they freeze up at multiple levels, then the mental becomes out of sync with the spinal, and therefore has to invent narratives. It includes self-aggrandizement. That is why we have to be careful when the mind glorifies itself or a part of itself. When we aggrandize artificial intelligence, we have entered a hall of mirrors.

I: We can become better and better at being worse and worse. Is that it?

A: The path to recuperation or emancipation may be entirely different than the conventional path of progress.

I: What does that mean at the pragmatic or pedagogical level?

A: Well, to begin with, we have to be existentially aware of the rhythms and cycles that constitute us. What are the minor and major convulsions taking place in us throughout the day and in sleep? These must needs be watched.

I: It helps in creating the dual view of ourselves as wave and particle, so to speak?

A: The particle is the symbolic aspect, and the wave is the cosmic dimension. They exist in reciprocal relation to each other.

I: But let us also speak of the second thing you mentioned among the ancients.

A: That is the sensitivity toward intuition, augury, and presentiment. We see it among the ancient Israelites. They were on the lookout for omens, portents, premonitions, and suchlike that seemed to indicate divine intent.

I: Surely we are not in an age where we can read the Hand of God?

A: No, we certainly are not. However, signs do not exist only in relation to divine providence. If I am watchful, I can see where life is taking me, where the resistances are, as well as the supports.

I: And what do I do with these?

A: I begin to formulate an alternate ground for evaluating my existential situation. I do not accept what society has taught me with respect to myself or the collective fantasies and narratives around me.

I: Ah, now I see what you are getting at. We can invent a new ground in which the two operating aspects are rhythm and portent.

A: There is a third thing, and that is love. Without love the other two are feeble.

I: Can we go into that a little bit?

A: When I lived in a different country, I looked at the earth and felt no pull. Here, back in my country of birth, I feel a strange sense of love for the soil. One must be where love is, and avoid where it is not.

I: So, rhythm, portent, and eros are the three basic predicates for creating an alternate ground of evaluation?

A: Pursued in an adequate manner, these weave an alternate plane that is no longer caught in the discourse of intelligence or any other prevailing discourse. As you can see, such a field is essentially independent of time, and gives a unique perspective.

I: What is the overall nature of this "field" then?

A: It is an energetic field, a passionate field that is brimming with life possibilities. We can call it the field of potentiality. It is Hope not because it is linked to tomorrow, but because it is linked to the cosmic dimension.

I: This "field" does not belong to any temporality or spatiality, but I may come in contact with it through my perspicacity. Would that be right?

A: I have to enter this field as it is gathering around me, intensifying in me, in a humble sort of way, without any presumptions. It is at the same time triggered by my concentrated efforts at participation, and yet is independent of me. Partaking of the field may be a good way to think about it.

I: So the mental and the elemental move us from individual relations to field relations which is a very different way to be in this world.

A: Very different. The thrust is not toward objectification, hierarchy, or dominance, but rather toward autonomy, enstrengthment, and potentiality.

I: From here we can put human characteristics like intelligence in perspective.

A: So we could, so we could. And we might find that unfortunately what we see is not pretty.

I: That may be so, but our field relations won't run the economy or be able to make rocket engines or high speed computing.

A: There is no claim to technical achievements. We are speaking of the other side of techne. It is meant as a critique of the present, only so as not to become too caught up in the social and its shifting practical needs.

I: But what's the good of it?

A: Recall the messianic warning: "Ye are the salt of this earth, but if the salt hath lost its savor, wherewith shall it be salted." Saltiness is not a characteristic of salt, but its selfnature seen from its own standpoint. Humans bereft of their selfnature are like salt without saltiness, fit to be discarded. Human beings in trouble do not think of rocket engines or computing. They withdraw into their little corner mostly unprepared for facing adversity. And then may come depression or a sense of futility.

I: So, this is adversity training? National disaster relief of some kind?

A: I can see you are getting impatient. Cynicism is not helpful either.

I: I'm merely trying to understand the usefulness of this kind of thinking.

A: Experimentation and advancement cannot happen only on the plane of material transformation. Other kinds of experiments have to go on side-by-side. I find myself stuck with this dense body … have to feed it, clothe it, and one day it simply starts to fall apart. So, what's going on? Should I remain a mute spectator busy only with computation and rocket engines, or should I attempt to find out what is going on with me at the existential level? Will artificial intelligence and public time save me from the meaningless void?

I: If I don't buy into the contemporary public discourse, I might get frustrated with this recalcitrant and muteness of life, and either indulge, abuse, or try to destroy myself, or attempt to destroy others from resentment.

A: But even extreme sophistication has no bearing on this. One of the greatest mathematicians of the present era, Kurt Gödel, starved himself to death because he believed that his food was being poisoned. Even Einstein's friendly remonstrations did not help.

I: An instantiation of the separation of the mental and the elemental that we discussed earlier? There are no privileged points it seems.

A: Isolated and separated, they produce phenomena; when brought together they illuminate *noumena*.

I: Yet both are necessary, otherwise we get stuck in a one-sided reality.

A: The field or "wave" view complements the particle or mental view. From here we can speak of mental attributes or accomplishments that are said to be intelligent.

I: In the field view, the body is compressed energy waves, and so intelligence as a measure appears as a fragment before it.

A: It may produce technological miracles, but they will always be alien to the other side. In other words, there is no direct enhancement of our lives, although it may result in power and prestige to the individual and the collective. But it cannot move into the other dimension. There we are all alone without amelioration.

I: Are you saying that despite the social approbation, achievements on the mental plane do not necessarily improve our lives?

A: It all depends on what we understand by improvement. If improvement means more and better ways of doing what we are doing, then there is improvement. But if improvement means a radical emancipatory insight into ourselves that helps us live freed lives, then perhaps not. Social forces not in our control keep us on tenterhooks consuming vast amounts of shock-absorbing emotional energy. This is so naturalized that we do not realize it. Improvement is usually construed within these parameters.

I: Which is no improvement at all, or only on certain counts and not on others.

A: We are not free to look and observe, caught as we are in different positionalities and ideological infirmities contrary to the cosmic. The cosmic is not in outer space, but in ourselves.

I: So could we say that true intelligence is the capacity to look and observe freely without preconceptions?

A: The shedding of anxieties is certainly one way of regaining health and perspective, by reconnecting to primal force fields.

I: And that is by means of the cultivation of the field of triadic elements—intuition, rhythm, and eros?

A: Cultivation is a good word. The continual interweaving of these three reconnects us to the force field of organic potentiality that is the ontological basis of meaningful existence.

I: So we are saying that there is social existence which is bound in the epistemic assumptions and presumptions of the time, which includes various discursive practices such as measurements including intelligence. Side-by-side, there is the ontological force field which constitute us at the elemental level with which one must develop familiarity.

A: Because if we don't, then there is a one-sided reality which is dangerous as it gives rise to illusions and delusions.

I: Coming back to the question of intelligence, are we now ready to say something definite about it?

A: We have been saying plenty on our way up to this point. But of course there is always more to be said. Accessing the ontological field gives you a sudden expansion from which a new language begins to emerge. This language may not coincide exactly with the solely mental apprehension that is in line with current thinking.

I: So you are saying that a certain language of description begins to emerge from this very act of dialogue, something not readily available.

A: When we are at the very edge of things, this is inevitable. We cannot understand things from the cold outside. We have to move in and warm up to the topic gradually. There is no easy path from the knowledge of the mental to the perception of the elemental, that is, the dual aspect of ourselves. But after a point, there is intuition, like with anything else.

I: Is intuition intrinsic to intelligence?

A: Is intuition intrinsic to art, is intuition intrinsic to physics? Intuition is not something separate from the quality of our being-in-the-world. Our elemental being resonates with the world, and it is this order of apprehension, when we are open to it, that we call intuition. A sensitive instrument resonates, a dull one does not.

I: I think we have stumbled upon something significant here. A growing intuition can connect the mental and the elemental.

A: We have to pay close attention to the world, moving from fact to fact, and not as we want things to be.

I: But usually intelligence is deemed to be that which helps us make the physical world conform to the way we want things to be. If it is warm, then we want to make it cool, if it is cold then we want to warm things up. If it is distant, then we want to bring it closer, and vice versa.

A: Physical manipulations of the material dimension will and must go on. Even some animals do that. But such adaptations do not mean anything more than that.

I: By that you mean, we are not intrinsically getting any better, in any absolute sense.

A: Better in the sense healthier, happier, or more perceptive? No, we are not.

I: But you would agree that we are getting more specialized. And that is perhaps part of being intelligent, I mean as a society?

A: Specialization is alright if there is intense cooperation, like within the organic body. But specialization in a highly competitive environment can spell disaster. Imagine the kidney competing with the spleen for oxygen.

I: So are you saying that one basic condition for ameliorative emancipation, if such a thing is akin to a perceived intelligent objective, is cooperation.

A: Surely attrition or attenuation cannot be a social objective? If it is not, then cooperation is a prerequisite.

I: So it seems that we have arrived at our quest indirectly, through elimination, analogy, and subversion.

A: Something begins to emerge, not as a definition of anything, but as the condition of its possibility.

I: We are almost saying that intelligence is emergent, rather than something pre-decided. That is somewhat scary. It means that we cannot go by any strictly objective criteria. What is intelligent behavior in one context may not be so in another.

A: There can be no fixed measure or method of arriving at a quotient that is always meaningful. You can be part of a high-IQ society such as Mensa, and yet act like an imbecile in other areas of life. There is absolutely no guarantee that solving artificial logical problems on a screen or a sheet of paper has anything to do with the phenomenology of lived situations, or that it prepares one to act intelligently in world relations.

I: Is that because living situations are multidimensional whereas pen and paper tests are one-dimensional?

A: It is not about difference in dimensionality, but about difference in orders. It is bit like the difference between knowing the science of kinesthetics and performing athletics on the field. These are differences of kind. I don't care what my Mensa score is, because I know that is not indicative of how I perform in the critical moments of life. The truly complex problems posed by lived life are not logical but ontological. These are of two different orders.

I: And yet we give tremendous importance to such scores.

A: Logic is only a derivative, an epiphenomenon. The people who have contributed most to human and planetary well-being may not even know what to do with an IQ test or even know such a thing exists.

I: So are we saying that such things as IQ tests do not measure anything real?

A: It all depends on what you mean by "real." If reality is defined by what can be arrived at step by step, then it certainly measures abilities to draw deductions, say, from axioms. But there are no inner steps to creative sensibility, or to love, or to fear, or anxiety, or even the capacity to manage complex human situations. There are no inner steps to intuition, and some of the most valuable exegeses of experience come from the sharpness of insight.

I: So we can say that IQ measured intelligence is always partial.

A: If you examine the four early papers of Einstein that eventually made him famous, you will find that the mathematics in them are no more sophisticated than high school level. But the interpretations and connections made in them are so profound as to be almost clairvoyant. Many can do the math, but only the sages will see the implications.

I: But insight, intuition, instinct, all of these are mystified terms, and not very helpful from an ordinary perspective.

A: That is so because we try to produce copies of each other. In actuality, each being is unique and there is no mystification if we are trained to follow our ken.

I: What you are saying is very significant because intrinsic to intelligence is the idea of homogeneity, otherwise there cannot be measurement.

A: A scale of measurement obviously implies relative rating. But the psyche is not calibrated uniformly, even within the same individual. Fear shrinks the psychic capacity, whereas love expands it. A child brought up under constant pressure is barely proprioceptive. A child brought up in genuine love is creative and free. Does it mean that the first child is less intelligent than the second one?

I: So this brings up yet another vital point. Intelligence is allied to the circumstances in which it is possible to be truthful or honest to oneself, just to be what one is.

A: And since this is immensely variable, our response to reality varies immensely, and not because of anything superior or inferior. Evolution has given us the variability, but we are busy trying to be like each other.

I: But a certain amount of uniformity is inevitable in a functional society, is it not?

A: Functional uniformity is different from psychic homogeneity. The French scholar Jacques Derrida had said that we have to hold meanings under erasure, because meanings are slippery.

I: Does that mean we have to simultaneously accept and reject a construct?

A: That is, I suppose, as close as we can get to his meaning. In the present case, intelligence, whatever that is, must be taken to be a snapshot from a particular direction within a specific set of circumstances. Change the circumstances radically, and you are likely to get a very different picture and result.

I: X feels very creative in the presence of Y, and quite otherwise in the presence of Z.

A: Some do very badly under pressure, others flourish under similar conditions.

I: So, intelligence is not something absolute. It depends on your assumptions and inclusions.

A: The channels you are willing to consider and activate. The number of frequencies you are willing to admit, and so on.

I: Given the arbitrariness of the construct, how useful is the notion of artificial intelligence?

A: It can certainly not be more useful than the base term.

I: It seems to suggest an efficient mimicking of the original.

A: Most of our advanced activities in the world are a mimicking of the natural, whether it is flying or cloning or integrated circuitry or computers.

I: I do not find that necessarily problematic. It widens the basis of human activities.

A: I did not say it was problematic. It was merely a statement of fact. Rather, what I am saying is that intelligence is already an artifice, a measured construct, as we have seen. So, then what exactly is an *artificial* artifice?

I: Electronic cloning or mimicking of organic data processing, which is what people usually mean by artificial intelligence or AI.

A: The primary purpose of organic intelligence is not data processing but meaning making.

I: But meaning cannot be defined in the domain of compu-tronics, only mechanical pattern recognition.

A: That is because there is no material meaning of meaning. Data processors, however sophisticated, are not meaning makers, they have no phenomenological intent or psychic content. They do what their designers and programmers intend them to do, nothing more, nothing less.

I: In other words, the intent is at once-remove, of a different order. Artificial Intelligence follows a blue-print, even if that blue-print is a constantly adjusting one, even if it is given status as learning or adaptive AI and so on.

A: Organic intelligence, on the other hand, is in search of surprise and its ground, that is, a break in the pattern that will unfold another level in evolution. We are mostly emotion, and only a fraction, processor. Emotions mostly guide the processing, and not the other way round. Without emotions we are nothing. Processing is a fairly recent thing. Ancient peoples hardly processed, but mainly absorbed whole patterns, resonated with the outside that guided them—the cosmic, that is.

I: Are you not giving too much importance to emotions?

A: Emotions are not what we think. It is impossible to *think* emotions, for they are prior to thought, by a long shot.

They are the motive power for growth and becoming. Feelings are just a small part of emotions.

I: But how then is intelligence connected to emotions?

A: It is not emotional intelligence or anything like that. That is baloney. This is the hardest part to grasp. One must learn to "surf" the emotions, and wait for the big one. The big one, when it comes, touches the right nerves where intelligence resides.

I: Where intelligence "resides?" How do you mean?

A: Living intelligence does not leave us, except at death.

I: So where does it reside?

A: Not where, but how. There is no localization, only an immanent process.

I: So intelligence is not hiding anywhere, but in plain sight. We only have to learn to "surf" the emotions in order to touch it?

A: It is in plain sight not in the sense of eyesight but within plain reach.

I: Yes, I understand that. It was only a manner of speaking.

A: And besides, the more you "surf," the higher you reach in terms of emotive power. And then, occasionally the big one makes the break.

I: "Makes the break?"

A: Touches the transmission line of living intelligence. This is what the Christ was referring to when he said "Man does not live by bread alone."

I: So, ordinarily, in spite of ourselves, we live by a trickle of this intelligence, and occasionally we are enabled to go beyond?

A: Occasionally, if we are so inclined, we seek and come in touch with the larger source.

I: What is the purpose of such an activity?

A: Purpose? Did you not begin by asking what is intelligence?

I: That seems so distant now.

A: I warned you that we need to gradually build up the intensity to the topic. And that can take us very far indeed. There are no easy answers to these questions, only an expansion of awareness that makes answers superfluous.

I: And it is also worth noting that we did not introduce any new idea or distant concept to come this far. What we have been doing essentially is digging deeper into what is already there.

A: There is me and you as individuals, and there is that high voltage transmission hovering above and around us from where we are drawing the current of life. And death is nothing but becoming unhooked from that circuit.

I: And how much we can draw depends on our circuitry?

A: On how evolved it is. Intelligence lies in this capacity to draw, to become neurologically fit to shift our level to upper circuits.

I: It is a physico-psychic upgradation, so to speak.

A: Absolutely. The neurological body needs to be fit to withstand the shock of anonymous autonomy that comes from higher intensities.

I: Wow, that's quite a mouthful! What on earth is "anonymous autonomy?"

A: First, the body must get used to being a nobody.

I: That's faintly paradoxical: a body becoming a no body?

A: That is, not identifying as this body or that body. Nobody is equivalent to anybody and everybody. That is the meaning of anonymity. I may be socially pinpointed as a named body, but that is only a functional matter.

I: But that is more psychological than physical, is that not so?

A: The body too gets imprinted with the image we have of ourselves. The psyche and the soma are part of a continuum and not isolates. We have to get away from the habits of the body associated with a somebody.

I: There is a kind of freedom in being a nobody … we are nobodies anyways.

A: And freedom is one of the conditions of possibility for intelligence.

I: Such as freedom from fear?

A: No, not freedom from anything, just freedom. Freedom from something is a relative thing, whereas freedom *per se* is inner expansion, the way things cool down, for instance.

I: We are now in a better position to take the concluding steps. These have to do with the discourse of AI and its positioning with regard to education.

A: What is AI but a representation of a representation—digital reconstruction of mental construction, an approximation of an approximation.

I: So there is no problem with AI so long as one understands the facts?

A: I do not understand your question.

I: With the background of AI, a lot of questions have been raised recently with regard to conventional education. The main thrust of these questions seems to be concerning the relevance of traditional education. The focus of schooling is mostly on the development of basic logic and literacy, which machines are able to do better. So the question seems to be: what is the future of conventional education and the skills it is able to impart, now that AI is here?

A: Both natural language and mathematical language are not primary. What is primary is experience, which is non-verbal. Education ought to focus on experience, that's all. AI does not have the experience of loving or nurturing or feeling lost; it can only make selections on the *descriptions* of these activities. But the description is never the described.

I: So, you're saying that the primarily descriptive focus of conventional education is wrong. That's the root of the confusion.

A: The mind has to continually *un*learn through authentic experience, in order to be truly educated. Because education is not something done and dusted. It is continual creative becoming.

I: But I still don't fully comprehend the difference between cybernetic learning including feedback systems and organic learning. Is the difference qualitative or merely quantitative?

A: The answer to your question lies in the Socratic dialogues of Plato.

I: If I recall correctly, Socrates regards all learning as awakening.

A: So, there's your difference. What can cybernetics awaken to, except electrical current?

I: But for that one must accept the Socratic view of learning.

A: Socrates was merely demonstrating that learning is not the acquisition of some alien facts, but must logically reside within us, albeit in some ordinarily inaccessible manner.

I: In other words, what we call learning is in actuality a partial awaking to what is already in us.

A: The difference is that each of us are in a different state of awaking, that's all. That is why the world resonates differently in us.

I: But that makes all the usual talk about intelligence nonsensical.

A: If that is so, then so be it.

I: But that is not very helpful. The world is being flooded with AI.

A: Machines can be made to learn through feedback that mimics human abilities, but only organic intelligence can be educated.

I: Okay, so that's a major step in making a distinction. Machines can learn, but only humans can be educated. And the difference lies in ...?

A: The difference between learning and education is that the first is acquisitive, and the second is normative. The first can be mimicked, but not the latter.

I: Normative?

A: There are ontological norms built into the organism. It is what the Vedic Indians called *Dharma*. One is educated or awakened according to one's *Dharma* or innate path of evolution. I won't attempt to go further into the term here, it is too complex.

I: As with the Socratic view, the sense of awakening is reaffirmed here. The machine has no *Dharma*, whereas the organism does.

A: The machine can only move from the known to the known, or react according to its learning, whereas the organism moves from the unknown to the known.

I: Can you explain "unknown to the known?"

A: We do not know our source, that is obvious. We merely find ourselves as such, thrust into the world, as Martin Heidegger once put it.

I: So the human and the machine, however sophisticated, are of two completely different orders.

A: Absolutely different. It's utterly uneducated to talk of machine intelligence versus human intelligence. As the machine advances, the human retreats, not in the sense of ceding ground, but in the sense of moving to higher ground. There is infinite surplus, and no machine can eat it all up.

I: To be educated is also to understand this radical difference, should that not be the case?

A: That is what intelligence is all about, to know the place of each thing.

I: Wow! If you had said that at the beginning, it would not have made much sense, or it would have become trivialized.

A: Of course, of course. That is why one must resist the urge to define everything quickly. Rather, one must break down the definitions, and look inside them.

I: In postmodern theory, they call it deconstruction.

A: Postmodern theory lacks ontological empathy, and is therefore hollow.

I: You could be intellectually lynched for saying that.

A: That would be welcome. I have a colleague who is a postmodern theorist; does not believe in Presence or Voice or anything that has a whiff of the ontological. Everything apparently deconstructs. And yet he fought a hard and bitter courtroom battle for child custody. Somehow, deconstruction does not seem to have any bearing on life situations. It is only good for lecturing in classrooms or for learned erudition in academic journals.

I: Are you accusing academia of hypocrisy?

A: Certainly of a kind of doublespeak in which word and practice seem to be asynchronous.

I: I cannot disagree. Since you mention asynchrony, I would like to come back to the question of rhythm. Intelligent field is predicated upon rhythm, eros, and the esoteric sign. Would you say that these elements heighten the sense of the Unknown from where we emerge?

A: These are, in fact, the holy triad of our entry into the world. We are born under a celestial sign, into parental eros, and held by a metabolic rhythm.

I: And intelligence, where does that figure?

A: Intelligence lies in bringing all of these into fine coordination. It is the actualization of potential. The more intense it is, the better.

I: Machine intelligence has no potential, meaning anything hidden, ununderstood sources, only the expressed actual-plus; but organic intelligence possesses potential since it is the unfoldment of the unknown. We do not know when the great artistic moment will come, or whether the mathematical breakthrough will happen.

A: Surprise! Ultimately, intelligence is emergent, not programmed. Look, a baboon or an orangutan cannot be programmed to become a human. It can be made to ape a human or mimic some gestures. But it cannot write *War and Peace*, or understand the *Sermon on the Mount*. No one knows when, or from where anthropic consciousness burst on the scene.

I: Agreed. What we have established so far is that AI is mechanical and not an extension of the organic, because these belong to two different orders. We have also established that learning is not education.

A: Education means to become involved in caring for the world and its relations. Learning is a mere empirical aspect of being in the world.

I: One must be awakened to education, but can be trained or programed to learn.

A: Thus the phrase 'learned but not educated.'

I: It presses upon us the inevitable conclusion that the world can be continually expanded or differentiated through learning, but it cannot be bettered.

A: Betterment is a function of wholeness; fragments of learning cannot lead to the sense of wholeness.

I: But we are not dismissing AI either.

A: How can we dismiss what is already there? AI is real and here to stay.

I: So, how is a balance obtained?

A: Between fragments and wholeness? There is no balance. Some of us will tilt one way, others will go the other way.

I: So the world will always be divided, torn, between these two poles?

A: It has always been the case, and it is safe to assume that it will always be so.

I: What about those who want to go beyond this conflict and duality?

A: Once we understand the premise of education well and become firmly established in it, then we can emerge any-time into the other side, as also withdraw at will. The converse is not possible.

I: You are saying that we can move from wholeness to the differentiated experience of the empirical world, but not the other way around. Why?

A: There is no mechanism that can put the fragments together and achieve wholeness. Differentiation can only lead to further differentiation.

I: So how can we hope to get to education?

A: Through negation.

I: Learning is a positive movement, and education is a negative one?

A: Negative in the sense you perceive or are led to perceive the limits of all reality. These limits are not easily achieved, but come out of rigorous inquiry.

I: And thus we sit at the edge of reality like at the edge of a canyon.

A: And watch the cerebro-spinal movements that connect the mental to the elemental. These movements become more pronounced at such limit points. The psychic-creative forces get excited.

I: So education becomes a spontaneous process?

A: If one can get this far, yes.

I: And the key raw material of education turns out to be emotional energy.

A: Passion. Education is pulsation—creative expansion and contraction, not imagery or verbal representation.

I: Expansion and contraction of what?

A: Of space.

I: What is the content and purpose of education then?

A: Integrative and creative well-being.

I: For the individual?

A: The individual and beyond.

I: And learning can be considered a subset of this endeavor?

A: Learning is necessary but not sufficient.

I: Not sufficient for what?

A: For a mature human life working toward fulfilment.

I: And machines are limited to learning. I'm just clarifying.

A: Absolutely limited, however sophisticated.

I: But people speak of enslavement to the machine. How do you see that?

A: One can be enslaved to anything, even to drugs. But is that, or should that, be the norm?

I: Okay, so slavery is simply not the point.

A: Machines are digital, and therefore verbal, of whatever kind. They cannot enter the non-verbal space.

I: So the fundamental difference lies in creative autonomy. Machines can ape the human, be an extension of the human, even destroy the human, but never be human.

A: One is the product of the mental, the other is the product of the elemental. The mental is simply epiphenomenal, a bye-product.

I: It is often alleged that humans are becoming like machines. It is the earlier argument turned on its head.

A: If one limits experience to learning one is bound to be machine-like. It is the refusal to be educated that is making people mechanical.

I: Is there a problem in that?

A: Visit any psychiatric hospital or clinic and you will find out.

I: You are implying that the exclusive focus on learning, and the non-consideration of education, leads to mental illnesses. Is that it?

A: If you exercise only one part of the human, and ignore the rest, then the latter will languish to the detriment of the whole. That is inevitable.

I: Where shall we locate intelligence in all of this?

A: Organic intelligence is like a catalyst, an invisible hand, everywhere and nowhere, spread throughout the being; whereas, AI, including machine learning, is an input-output device. These are qualitatively different things.

I: If you were forced to choose between a driver-driven car and a self-driven car, which would you choose and why?

A: Well, motion in public spaces involves ethical decisions, however minor, simply because there are others around. And machines cannot make ethical decisions.

I: They can make logical decisions but not ethical ones. And this brings us back to the question of education and its connection to intelligence.

A: Intelligence, whether of the organic kind or its analog in the machinic kind, can make hydrogen bombs or thorium engines, space colonies or oceanic ones, but none of these can be accommodated in the psyche. These will always remain as external phenomena. And such being the case, my psyche will remain unresolved by what is going on outside, filled with unknown terrors and anxieties, just like in the millions of generations before us.

I: So, intelligence has no impact on the psyche.

A: No, not even of the Einsteinian kind. Einstein was deeply worried about the human condition and its future direction. He frequently mentioned God and was deeply religious. It hardly requires mention that Einstein's God was not of any church or denomination. It was the cosmic connection and the ethical channels bred out of it.

I: If it is not intelligence, then what will emancipate the psyche?

A: Nothing. The psyche is not there to be emancipated. It can be silenced but not emancipated. Silence will make the cosmic rhythm manifest itself.

I: But there must be some middle ground with which we can live. Silencing the psyche is not an option for most of us.

A: That is where education comes in. Education is the dynamic ground generated by the connection between the psyche and the elemental. It is not something fixed by a curriculum. It is the slow liberation-expansion of the elemental forces guided by ethics. That is why, to be educated is to be unique. One can pick up a trick or two on the side.

I: In other words, education is not curriculum-bound or capability-bound.

A: Let us say, you need to get to the top of a mountain. You can get there on mule-back, by trekking, or by rope-way, it does not matter. The rope or the mule are only incidental.

I: Education helps to get us beyond the schizophrenic split between civilizational life and psychic life, the split that Freud had identified way back, and that had made him despondent. Intelligence is not in the picture. But the point is, how can we help as educators?

A: Get yourself educated first.

I: Well, huh? Well I guess you are right. Otherwise it is the blind leading the blind.

A: Intelligence leads you into differentiation; education leads you out of it. Both these movements must go on side-by-side.

I: This is a new kind of schizophrenia you are proposing.

A: The schizophrenia is already there. I'm merely trying to find a way to deal with it.

I: A sort of double consciousness that Freud could not admit?

A: Freud did see the absurdity and inadequacy of what goes by the name of education. But he did not seem to have suggested anything other than saying that we send out students into the wintry night dressed in summer clothes, or some such thing alluding to the inadequacy.

I: Has anyone else thought further along these lines?

A: Rudolf Steiner made some important observations in his lectures and writings in the early part of the previous century. So did Annie Besant. A third name that comes to mind is Sri Aurobindo, the Indian thinker. All of these folks, stretched well beyond the learning paradigm of education and touched upon the awakening paradigm. They did not deny the learning aspect, but inquired about the ground of learning, which cannot be identical.

I: Thus it seems we have arrived at an important difference. The important distinction from the point of view of education is not between natural intelligence and artificial intelligence, but between intelligence as a category, and the ground of intelligence, from whose intuitive touch we get a sense of purpose for intellection.

A: That's a reasonable way to summarize a difficult discussion. But now you see why it took us so many steps to arrive at this realization.

I: We had to move the focus from one kind of hiatus to a different one. One might even say, from a false distinction to a real one. But now I want to ask a different question. Is this ground of intelligence what one might call God?

A: For me, God is not a reality or a category, but the ground of every knowing. In other words, God is not knowable because it is the ground of all knowing.

I: So all attempts at objectifying God is fruitless. Does that imply we can leave it out of the conversation?

A: It is included in every conversation, whether implicitly or explicitly, whether in affirmation or denial.

I: Coming back to artificial intelligence one final time, can we say that it has a future especially in education?

A: Having a future or not having a future is not a measure of anything fundamental. Both kitsch and cockroaches have a future. The question is: what is the quality of that future? Is that future headed toward technocratic narcissism or toward ethico-aesthetic emancipation?

CHAPTER 6

Intelligence and the *Threptikon*

As we approach the concluding pages of this inquest into intelligence, a categorical distinction shows up before us that is impossible to ignore, and one that will be constitutive of the most important closing statement of this book. This distinction that now stares at us in the face is not in the nature of an opposition but of a kind of complementarity. Intelligence as a range of socially relevant capacities linked to a plethora of identifiable tasks, their systemic linkages, and systematic solution paths may be called a publicality or an intelligence system linked to the decision paths of a state of society. In so far as the individual is concerned, they are hooked to this publical intelligence, that includes the knowledge system and the reward system, through feeding on collective continuity, or the sense of an unending public time mixed up with private aspiration. In other words, existential meaning or significance under whose aura cognitive phenomena such as intelligence discursively attain their status, in turn, comes from the unconscious internalization of an apparently continuous temporal extension (in which identity seemingly continues as part of an indefinite temporal river), and its projected hopes of a future.

But this dream of indefinite time is ruptured when the individual comes up against the facticity of transience through a variety of non-public and internal experiences—the collective time and its durational accomplishments seem to wither away, replaced by a different set of anxieties, including the anxiety of non-being. As soon as the private discontinuity becomes

K. Roy, *Education, "Artificial" Intelligence, and Cognition*,
https://doi.org/10.1007/978-3-031-82263-6_6

real to the individual, the illusions bred of the publicality or collective continuity begins to fall apart, and a personal nothingness begins to lurk in the shadows of consciousness no longer eased by the assurances of a rising atmosphere of simulated capabilities. Questions such as "what's the point of it all," or "why even bother" gradually get to get a toehold in thought. This is the time-bound identity shorn of the comfortable illusion of indefiniteness borne on the back of artifice. All of a sudden the finish line appears not too far ahead, and all the accumulated cultural meanings and valuable intelligences seem like a mirage, withdrawing into the distance. A revised view of existence and its temporality becomes warranted in the face of this apparent nothingness that stares at the individual.

> This does not mean, however, that humans are not, and do not have to be something, that they are simply consigned to nothingness and therefore can freely decide whether to be or not to be, to adopt or not to adopt this or that destiny (nihilism and decisionism coincide at this point). There is in effect something that humans are and have to be, but this something is not an essence nor properly a thing: It is the simple fact of one's own existence as possibility or potentiality. But precisely because of this things become complicated; precisely because of this ethics becomes effective. Since the being most proper to humankind is being one's own possibility or potentiality, then and only for this reason (that is, insofar as humankind's most proper being—being potential—is in a certain sense lacking, insofar as it can not be, it is therefore devoid of foundation and humankind is not always already in possession of it), humans have and feel a debt. Humans, in their potentiality to be and to not-be, are, in other words, always already in debt; they always already have a bad conscience without having to commit any blameworthy act. This is all that is meant by the old theological doctrine of original sin.[1]

Thus we arrive at something that we might call organic or sentient intelligence, in order to distinguish it from the exteriorized and purely data-based category. The above lines sketch out the issue facing this sentient intelligence very nicely. If public continuity is not the individual's intimate destiny, then what must an individual do in order to awaken to the intelligence proper to her or him? This is the vital pedagogical question that ought to engage the coming community—the need to become real to one's actual and intimate destiny shorn of public fantasy. It leads to

[1] Giorgio Agamben, *The Coming Community* (Minneapolis: University of Minnesota Press, 1993), p. 42.

the realization that there is self-nature that is prior to all knowledge (public induction) and reflexivity (internalized fantasy); to remain in denial or ignorance of it is in the nature of original sin. Ethics is this study of duplicity that is born of empiricism, and a potential turn toward simply being. The investigation into the ethical responsibility of being is the investigation into private or reserve intelligence shorn of the reference to the social or collective forms. And this means delving directly into human potentiality, for being *is* potentiality, a pure urgent vitality of no-thingness that wells up within.

> Morality, on the other hand, refers this doctrine to a blameworthy act humans have committed and, in this way, shackles their potentiality, turning it back toward the past. The recognition of evil is older and more original than any blameworthy act, and it rests solely on the fact that, being and having to be only its possibility or potentiality, humankind fails itself in a certain sense and has to appropriate this failing-it has to exist as potentiality. Like Perceval in the novel by Chretien de Troyes, humans are guilty for what they lack, for an act they have not committed. This is why ethics has no room for repentance; this is why the only ethical experience (which, as such, cannot be a task or a subjective decision) is the experience of being (one's own) potentiality, of being (one's own) possibility-exposing, that is, in every form one's own amorphousness and in every act one's own inactuality. The only evil consists instead in the decision to remain in a deficit of existence, to appropriate the power to not-be as a substance and a foundation beyond existence; or rather (and this is the destiny of morality), to regard potentiality itself, which is the most proper mode of human existence, as a fault that must always be repressed.[2]

The vulgar version of ethics is morality that turns an omission into an act of commission, and creates confusion by ascribing this lack of being-as-potentiality to a positive act (of evil). That which remains as human potential can be regained at any instant and does not require any form of repentance or looking back. In order to re-locate ourselves in potentiality, the coming community does not have to do anything—it is not a task or decision based achievement. It is simply the experience of being one's own potentiality, that which is the most intimate of experiences. The only evil inheres in remaining in ignorance of being resulting in a "deficit of existence." In simply being, there is no time or substance, no history or

[2] Ibid., p. 43.

society, which is probably why it needs to be repressed in mass society. It needs to be repressed also because the collective or public intelligence cannot ultimately sustain the individual, but the resultant deficit of existence can be exploited, in the manner of compensatory issuing of endless temporal credit (cards, hope, etc.). The denial of this false perpetuity—an illusion born of the psychologization of physical progression—properly alludes to a radically different realization. Education works very hard at preventing such a realization, albeit unconsciously, and keeps the mind tracked along publicalities (such as AI), for discussions of ethicality may not be good for economics.

> There is a well-known parable about the Kingdom of the Messiah that Walter Benjamin (who heard it from Gershom Scholem) recounted one evening to Ernst Bloch, who in turn transcribed it in Spuren: "A rabbi, a real cabalist, once said that in order to establish the reign of peace it is not necessary to destroy everything nor to begin a completely new world. It is sufficient to displace this cup or this bush or this stone just a little, and thus everything. But this small displacement is so difficult to achieve and its measure is so difficult to find that, with regard to the world, humans are incapable of it and it is necessary that the Messiah come." Benjamin's version of the story goes like this: "The Hassidim tell a story about the world to come that says everything there will be just as it is here. Just as our room is now, so it will be in the world to come; where our baby sleeps now, there too it will sleep in the other world. And the clothes we wear in this world, those too we will wear there. Everything will be as it is now, just a little different." There is nothing new about the thesis that the Absolute is identical to this world. It was stated in its extreme form by Indian logicians with the axiom, "Between Nirvana and the world there is not the slightest difference." What is new, instead, is the tiny displacement that the story introduces in the messianic world. And yet it is precisely this tiny displacement, this "everything will be as it is now, just a little different," difficult to explain. This cannot refer simply to real circumstances, in the sense that the nose of the blessed one will become a little shorter, or that the cup on the table will be displaced exactly one-half centimeter, or that the dog outside will stop barking. The tiny displacement does not refer to the state of things, but to their sense and their limits. It does not take place in things, but at their periphery, in the space of ease between every thing and itself. This means that even though perfection does not imply a real mutation it does not simply involve an external state of things, an incurable "so be it." On the contrary, the parable introduces a possibility there where everything is perfect, an "otherwise" where everything is finished forever, and precisely this is its irreducible

aporia. But how is it possible that things be "otherwise" once everything is definitively finished?[3]

Between paradise and hell there is not a whole lot, but only a small change in the angle of vision. This tiny displacement or difference-which-is-not-a-difference that makes the same appear new comes to be when we see the world through the luminosity of our potentiality. This potentiality must not be mistaken for some material or non-material becoming or enhancement. In fact, there exists no positive description of it since there is no gap between ourselves and our potentiality—only in separation can there be an effort at description. Looked at from the other side, when is phenomena not able to carry us away or destabilize us? It is when we have found ourselves back in potentiality. In potentiality there is no time because there is no progression, and therefore everything is the same and yet not the same; each thing appears in its true significance with regard to every other thing, accompanied by the removal of anxiety associated with existential deficit which is time and progression. This is the curative "movement Plato describes as erotic anamnesis, a movement that transports the object not toward another thing or another place, but toward its own taking-place."[4] The movement toward another thing, idea, symbol, or solution is the act of public or systemic induction, whereas, the recall or remembrance of pure being is erotic anamnesis, the backing into organic intelligence. We venture to say that it is this movement of eros that inheres in anamnesis which is central to the absolute realization of human intelligence, the one that eliminates existential deficit. In other words, it is the regaining of one's "own taking-place," or perhaps what Heidegger had called *Dasein*—the fullness experienced in simply *being there*. It is not dependent on any extensionality or any characteristic of the times, and therefore simply free to be, as an uncommitted organic vitality.

However, is this anamnesis to be regarded as individual or communitarian or something else? For in this final chapter, as educators we need to make a commitment to the becoming of the collective. Further, following the word "community" in the title, we feel obliged to establish a connection between what appears as the becoming-intelligent of the individual and its relation to the collective becoming, without which the apparent privatization of intelligence could be seen as a kind of solipsistic

[3] Ibid., p. 53.
[4] Ibid., p. 2.

mystification shorn of larger significance. In order to understand this equation, it is imperative that we take a closer look at the relation between the individual and the collective from the perspective of our central problematic.

> The antinomy of the individual and the universal has its origin in language. The word "tree" designates all trees indifferently, insofar as it posits the proper universal significance in place of singular ineffable trees *(terminus supponit significatum pro re)*. In other words, it transforms singularities into members of a class, whose meaning is defined by a common property (the condition of belonging 'ε'). The fortune of set theory in modern logic is born of the fact that the definition of the set is simply the definition of linguistic meaning. The comprehension of singular distinct objects *m* in a whole M is nothing but the name. Hence the inextricable paradoxes of classes, which no "beastly theory of types" can pretend to solve. The paradoxes, in effect, define the place of linguistic being. Linguistic being is a class that both belongs and does not belong to itself, and the class of all classes that do not belong to themselves is language. Linguistic being (being-called) is a set (the tree) that is at the same time a singularity (*the* tree, *a* tree, *this* tree); and the mediation of meaning, expressed by the symbol ε, cannot in any way fill the gap in which only the article succeeds in moving about freely.[5]

In discovering and locating ourselves in singularity there is both individuality and community. The separation is mainly linguistic grouping coming out of a characteristic of language. The singularity of being opens out unto both individuality and trans-individuality because singularity is not the attribute of any personality but is in the manner of a generative passage between them. It is thus *devoid of symbolic or linguistic content* as such and more of the form of an intensity or a moving existential hotspot whose main quality (if one may even use that word) is a weightless freedom that is not freedom from anything.

> [Some] medieval philosophers held that the passage from potentiality to act, from common form to singularity, is not an event accomplished once and for all, but an infinite series of modal oscillations. The individuation of a singular existence is not a punctual fact, but a *linea generationis substantiae* that varies in every direction according to a continual gradation of growth and remission, of appropriation and impropriation. The image of the line is

[5] Ibid., p. 8.

> not gratuitous. In a line of writing the *ductus* of the hand passes continually from the common form of the letters to the particular marks that identify its singular presence, and no one, even using the scrupulous rigor of graphology, could ever trace the real division between these two spheres. So too in a face, human nature continually passes into existence, and it is precisely this incessant emergence that constitutes its expressivity. The passage from potentiality to act, from language to the word, from the common to the proper, comes about every time as a shuttling in both directions along a line of sparkling alternation on which common nature and singularity, potentiality and act change roles and interpenetrate. The being that is engendered on this line is whatever being, and the manner in which it passes from the common to the proper and from the proper to the common is called usage, or rather, *ethos*.[6]

Just as the line passes continually into the forms of the letters (through the hand), giving them their singular presence, human potentiality too continually passes into existence with an "incessant emergence." It is not a once-for-all act, but a ceaseless coming-to-be. This ceaseless coming-to-be is the movement from potentiality to the expressivity of life, one which produces not the individual but a singularity, a "whatever-being." This whatever-being is the bridge between individuality and community. The intelligence proper to whatever-being is not a task or individuality or knowledge based one, but a creative movement between the particular and the genus. It represents the pure vitality of anonymous elan without the recuperation of which the human is reduced to cultural kitsch pointing toward species irrelevance.

> This means that the planetary petty bourgeoisie is probably the form in which humanity is moving toward its own destruction. But this also means that the petty bourgeoisie represents an opportunity unheard of in the history of humanity that it must at all costs not let slip away. Because if *instead of continuing to search for a proper identity in the already improper and senseless form of individuality*, humans were to succeed in belonging to this impropriety as such, in making of the proper being—thus not an identity and an individual property but a *singularity without identity*, a common and absolutely exposed singularity—if humans could, that is, not be-thus in this or that particular biography, but be only *the* thus, their singular exteriority and their face, then they would for the first time enter into a community without presuppositions and without subjects, into a communication

[6] Ibid., p. 10.

> without the incommunicable. Selecting in the new planetary humanity those characteristics that allow for its survival, removing the thin diaphragm that separates bad mediatized advertising from the perfect exteriority that communicates only itself—this is the political task of our generation.[7]

The coming community is both at the edge of destruction through bourgeoisfication, and at the same time at the cusp of a breakthrough beyond petty bourgeois identity. Here then is the crux of the matter—residing in the possibility of a *singularity sans individuality* is the essence of intelligence of the not-public and not-private kind. It is the intelligence of the whatever-being that unites the individual and the collective, that is not symbolic or representational, and that passes from genus to species and back from species to genus, something that Marx had intuited as *Gattungswesen*, a German word often translated as species-being. This singularity, or species-being passing-into-expression, is free of the burden of individuality or personality based identity, thus by-passing the society of kitsch. With the discovery of whatever-being or anonymous identity, the pedagogical ground is laid for the *threptikon* or the nutritive life that eliminates existential deficit. It is also the bridge between being and non-being, which eliminates the fear factor. Taken together, this is the highest form of sentient intelligence in which the latter becomes both the means and the end to species being.

But let us focus briefly on the term *threptikon*, or more particularly, the notion of *psychic threptikon* as an adapted form for our purpose.

> For Aristotle, the soul is one, but endowed with five groups of faculties (*dunameis*): the faculty (*threptikon*) concerned with the maintenance and development of organic life; the appetite (*opektikon*), or the tendency to any good; the faculty of sense perception (*aisthetikon*); the "locomotive" faculty (*kinetikon*), which presides over the various bodily movements; and reason (*dianoetikon*). The Scholastics generally follow Aristotle's classification. For them body and soul are united in one complete substance. The soul is the *forma substantialis*, the vital principle, the source of all activities. Hence their science of the soul deals with functions which nowadays belong to the provinces of biology and physiology. In more recent times, however, especially under the influence of Descartes, the mind has been separated, and even estranged, from the organism. Psychology deals only with the inner world, that is, the world of consciousness and its conditions. The nature of

[7] Ibid., p. 65, italicization mine.

> the mind and its relations to the organism are questions that belong to philosophy or meta-physics. As a consequence, also, modern psychology fails to distinguish between the spiritual faculties of the soul, i.e. those which the soul exercises itself without the intrinsic cooperation of the organism, and the faculties of the compositum, i.e. the soul and organism united in one complete principle of action, or of one special animated organ.[8]

In Aristotle, the *threptikon* is the vital power of self-maintenance in the organism ensuring against the tendency of matter to disintegrate. We might call it the binding force of the living organism. But what of the mind-consciousness, what binds it together that can sustain a meaningful psycho-affective response to the world? Of course nothing binds it together, and that is why the individual is often at war with himself, immersed in conflict and self-contradiction in a manner that no machine could ever be. But just as contradiction is a limiting condition for the psyche, freedom from conflict is an emancipatory condition that is not available to the machinic order. And how is this achieved? There is no positive path to it, for otherwise it would be reduced to the mechanical order. Rather it consists of a negation of properties or characteristics of the social or personal order. One is thereby "freed from the false dilemma that obliges knowledge to choose between the ineffability of the individual and the intelligibility of the universal. The intelligible, according to a beautiful expression of Levi ben Gershon, is neither a universal nor an individual included in a series, but rather singularity insofar as it is whatever-singularity. In this conception, such-and-such being is released from its having this or that property, which identifies it as belonging to this or that set, to this or that class, and it is reclaimed not for another class nor for the simple generic absence of any belonging, but for its *being-such,* for belonging to itself. Thus *being-such,* which remains constantly hidden in the condition of belonging ("there is an *x such that* it belongs to *y*") and which is in no way a real predicate, comes to light itself: The singularity exposed as such is whatever you *want,* that is, lovable."[9] In other words, the *psychic threptikon* is a state of love that is approached through jettisoning all predicates through which conflict, contradiction, and fragmentation arise and

[8] C. A. Dubray, "Encyclopedia: Faculties of the Soul" @ https://www.catholic.com/encyclopedia/faculties-of-the-soul.

[9] Agamben, op. cit., p. 1.

are maintained, resulting in a loss of vitality. Hence, the "binding force" of the psyche is nothing other than love freed of civilizational dross.

What pedagogic act then befalls us? On the existential side, it is to intimately understand the nature of the predicate that confounds psychic well-being with technique. This is the starting point of ethics.

> Ethics begins only when the good is revealed to consist in nothing other than a grasping of evil and when the authentic and the proper have no other content than the inauthentic and the improper. This is the meaning of the ancient philosophical adage according to which "veritas patefacit se ipsam et falsum." Truth cannot be shown except by showing the false, which is not, however, cut off and cast aside somewhere else. On the contrary, according to the etymology of the verb *patefacere,* which means "to open" and is linked to *spatium,* truth is revealed only by giving space or giving a place to non-truth—that is, as a taking-place of the false, as an exposure of its own innermost impropriety.[10]

One cannot teach the truth, for truth is nothing other than an absence of falsehood. Real intelligence consists not in casting away empirical attributes or falsehoods, but in grasping them completely as the inauthentic and the improper. This is the ethico-pedagogical task of sentient (human) intelligence. It brings us back to the point of erotic anamnesis or the psycho-somatic elevation recuperated by a return to whatever-being or pure identity.

When we place all of these momentous things next to that which is mind-invented, task-based, and simulated, there appears before us not a comparison between two things, but a dimensional difference between them. A rough analogy comes to mind—it is not unlike the juxtaposition of the Buddha or the Christ next to an actor who mimics these characters in front of the crowd or the camera—the authentic placed against the fake. What is required for a pedagogical understanding is the anamnesis, or the coming-to-be of what is. Eros in this context is an implosion that lifts the veil between exteriority and interiority leading to a phenomenological grasp of the fact that simulacra, which appear before us as independent and objectified, are nothing but the exteriorization of mediatized aspects of interiority. The pedagogical task of the coming community or planetary humanity is to go beyond mediatization, which also means to set aside all simulacra and artificiality in order to reach for the authentic. The

[10] Ibid., p. 12.

authentic is auto-poietic, and thus it is that we are responsible for giving birth to ourselves, to return to ourselves, not once, not twice, but again and again for attaining our threptic self-nature that is free of the empirical—in our self-nature there is no informational content.

But what of artificial intelligence, how shall we conceive of our relation to it? Let us begin by looking at some of the synonyms of the term artificial: false, fake, mock, non-natural, synthetic, imitation, and so on. None of it is flattering, and all of it is other than the authentic. It even appears oxymoronic when pre-fixed to intelligence. Language thus warns us of the dangers inherent in aritificiality. Nevertheless, fake or not, since AI is a form of social production we cannot dismiss it, but rather grasp its elements for pedagogical consideration. "According to current opinion, all of man's doing—that of the artist and the craftsman as well as that of the workman and the politician—is praxis, that is, manifestation of a will that produces a concrete effect. When we say that man has a productive status on earth, we mean, then, that the status of his dwelling on earth is a *practical* one."[11] However, at other times and among other cultures the highest form of human production was not necessarily conceived as a manifestation of the will or the production of concrete effects.

> The Greeks, to whom we owe all the categories through which we judge ourselves and the reality around us, made a clear distinction between *poiesis* (*poiein*, "to pro-duce" in the sense of bringing into being) and *praxis* (*prattein*, "to do" in the sense of acting). As we shall see, central to praxis was the idea of the will that finds its immediate expression in an act, while, by contrast, central to poiesis was the experience of pro-duction into presence, the fact that something passed from nonbeing to being, from concealment into the full light of existence. The essential character of poiesis was not its aspect as a practical and voluntary process but its being a mode of truth understood as unveiling, *aletheia*. And it was precisely because of this essential proximity to truth that Aristotle, who repeatedly theorizes this distinction within man's "doing," tended to assign a higher position to poiesis than to praxis.[12]

Beginning with early modernity, this important distinction between poiesis and praxis begins to lose its sharpness, ultimately vanishing in the works of thinkers such as John Locke, Adam Smith, and Karl Marx. Now,

[11] Giorgio Agamben, *The Man Without Content* (Stanford: Stanford University Press, 1999), p. 68.

[12] Ibid., p. 69.

the key to all value is labor, that is, praxis. The experience of aletheia or revealment or bringing to light becomes invisible. The double aspect of human existence is reduced to a single dimension. Work, that was once considered the domain of the subordinate, now ascends to the highest position as the producer of material wealth. Thus all things artificial begin to be thought of as "tributary to a determination of the essence of human activity as will and vital impulse, and are therefore founded in the forgetting of the original pro-ductive moment as foundation of the space of truth. The point of arrival of Western aesthetics is a metaphysics of the will, that is, of life understood as energy and creative impulse. ... And yet what the Greeks meant [by poiesis] was the production of truth and the subsequent opening of a world for man's existence."[13] Therefore it is not surprising that artificial intelligence has acquired this great purchase in the one-dimensional social imaginary during an epoch when the distinction between poiesis and praxis has been forgotten. This loss has enormous philosophical and existential consequences. At one level, it means that the production of the "space of truth" has been replaced and coopted by the production of material substance and task-oriented capabilities, giving rise to the hysterical enthusiasm for simulacra, or that which is fake or inauthentic by definition. Secondly, the abolished space of truth or poiesis is not something gratuitous; it is a necessity for healthy existence, whether for the individual or society as a whole. The non-empirical side of the human or the content-free aspect is just as important for the vital life as is the empirical side. Shrinkage of this space can and does have throttling consequences for the creative life. Thus we can say that "Man has on earth a poetic status, because it is *poiesis* that founds for him the original space of his world. Only because in the poetic *epoche* he experiences his being-in-the-world as his essential condition, does a world open up for his action and his existence. Only because he is capable of the most uncanny power, the power of pro-duction into presence, is he also capable of praxis, of willed and free activity. Only because he attains, in the poetic act, a more original temporal dimension is he a historical being, for whom, that is, at every instant his past and future are at stake."[14] Here we see a critical reversal: Marx had inferred that philosophy is not prior to history, whereas the present inquiry shows in multiple ways that poiesis is before praxis. The timeless is always prior to the temporal (not in the sense of sequence

[13] Ibid., p. 72.
[14] Ibid., p. 101.

but as inevitability), and it is the metaphysical dimension that opens up the world for willed activity, and not the other way round. Hence poietic *epoche* or bracketing of civilizational production becomes a necessary pedagogical action in order to bring into view that which is prior to civilizational praxis.

But there is more: even the willed activity and directed action is never straightforward, for its consequences, howsoever well thought out, do not always match the intended outcome or direction. The phrase "unintended consequences" thus politely acknowledges even while camouflaging many a troubling irony, making the latter appear as a fundamental condition of praxis. Irony thus attains special significance for our critique due to the fact that it opposes the literal and the figurative, the description and the explanation, the symbolic and the experiential, and the appearance and the actual. And what is crucial, it is only the embodied with its storehouse of the psychic life and inexplicable access to cultural archetypes that can grasp the allusion or the ironical reference. Machines or machinic capabilities are never ironical—it would result in operational breakdown due to the introduction of the self-contradictory in the logical and deductive processes. But let us make a minor excursus in order to grasp the serious consequences of the presence of irony in human communication and the manner of dealing with such a high order of complexity with minimum fuss.

> Cutler (1974, p.117) considers that an ironic utterance expresses a conveyed meaning which is the opposite, converse, or reverse of its literal meaning. Based on the classical definition of irony, Cutler (1974, p.117), in her article "On Saying What You Mean without Meaning What You Say," considers that an ironic utterance expresses a conveyed meaning which is the "opposite," "converse" or "reverse" of its literal meaning. She also states that the speaker produces this kind of utterance "by superimposing a certain intonation contour which signals to his hearers that the utterance is intended to be ironic." In his entry on irony, Abrams (1985, pp.97–100) defines nine categories and subcategories of irony—verbal, structural, stable and unstable, dramatic, tragic, cosmic, and romantic—along with comments upon several related terms (sarcasm, invective, and so on). Cutler (1974, p.119) makes a distinction between "spontaneous" and "provoked" irony. In the former, "the speaker is expressing what he/she means with no reference to previous context or conversation." The utterances belonging to the spontaneous category must be approbatory in the literal reading. On the other hand, in a "provoked irony", the speaker "repeats back to his audience something which the audience has previously said or held, with the ironic

intonation indicating that the previous claim has turned out to be wrong." Cutler states that a "provoked irony" also meets the "approbation condition."[15]

The utterance "Oh really," could be made to signify "Oh really?" (literal), or "Oh really! (exclamation), or "Oh really!!" (exasperation), or "Oh re..a..lly" (incredulity), and so on, depending on the intonation of the articulation. Human language is often not literal, assuming a whole host of meanings depending on the manner in which it is articulated, as well as the context in which it is articulated. There are often enunciations in which we actually mean the opposite of what we say, such as in the sarcastic "You're welcome ..." or "Please don't be bothered ...." The immense variations are cultural and organic, and cannot be mimicked by artificial means simply because the machine has no context for it, let alone approximate the affective source or inner life from which it emerges. In fact, the very aspects that make human language so rich and colorful, are not available to the non-organic and the non-sentient, and among these linguistic devices, irony is supreme. It attains a great poignancy when irony is directed at ourselves revealing an awareness of our uncertain ontological status.

> To be specific, irony is a literary term underlying different definitions and various categories by scholars from Socrates's era to the present. Among different theories proposed by different scholars, this paper will deal with the metaphor type postulated by Znamenskya (2004). According to Znamenskya (2004), there are three types of irony: situational irony, verbal irony and dramatic irony. (1) Situational irony: Irony of situation is a discrepancy between the expected result and actual results. It deals with the unexpected and the incoherent situations. It is embedded in an environment where the universe seems to be against you, in other words, when the unexpected happens. (Abrams 1985, p.97); (2) Verbal irony: Abrams (1985, p.97) argued that verbal irony is a statement in which the meaning that a speaker implies differs sharply from the meaning that is ostensibly expressed. The ironic statement usually involves the explicit expression of one attitude or evaluation, but with indications in the overall speech-situation that the speaker intends a very different and opposite attitude; (3) Dramatic irony: In Abrams' (1985, p.99) view dramatic irony involves a situation in which

[15] Myo Lwin, "Study of the Use of Irony Highlighted by Fictional Elements in the Short Story "*The Gift of the Magi*" by O. Henry," *Yangon University of Foreign Languages Research Journal 2020, Vol. 11, No.2*, pp. 213–220.

> the audience or readers shares with the author knowledge of present or future circumstances of which a character is ignorant; in that situation, the character unknowingly acts in a way we recognize to be grossly inappropriate to the actual circumstances, or expects the opposite of what we know that fates hold in store.[16]

But irony is not merely a literary device; it is much more than that. *Gulliver's Travels* is not merely literary amusement, but sardonic political commentary; *Crime and Punishment* is not just a moral dilemma, but the irony hidden in hubris; *Animal Farm* is not just allegorical comedy, but a severe political warning. What we find common is that irony is closely associated with ethics and its widespread use in literary works is only a reflection of its centrality in human praxeological relations. In sum, the presence of irony is the production of the "whatever being" that we saw earlier, because it engenders a line that is not logical progression but loops back on itself in a negative act that contradicts prior content. Only sentient intelligence associated with psychic or inner life is properly able to respond to irony, and travel beyond in the formation of ethos.

In conclusion, I wish to reiterate the finding of this inquiry that there is no comparison or competition between natural or sentient intelligence and artificial ones. As has been shown repeatedly by means of careful analysis in the foregoing pages of the book, they belong to very different ontological categories or planes. By technologically mimicking certain world-expressions of sentient intelligence, one cannot get to the secret of the latter—the existential root and purpose of poiesis is not the existential goal and meaning of techne or praxis. One cannot bring about the experience of revelation by stitching together all the descriptions, explanations, representations, and acts of revelation, any more than one can become creative by reading about creativity, or become a novelist by reading a novel. Of course, one can endlessly complicate the empirical world, increase its velocity, expand its scope, and magnify its spectacular-ness, but there is no willed path to the natural. Such a crossover is ontologically impossible, and whoever claims to the contrary will end up simply misleading the coming community. All the Turing machine talk about the artificial variety equaling the human (natural) or even surpassing the latter is rich fantasy coming out of the historical blunder of invisibilizing the poietic dimension of existence, and reducing it to praxis. The pedagogic

[16] Ibid., p. 214.

task before the coming community is clear—it is to recuperate and maintain a phenomenological distinction between poiesis and praxis such that each living moment we can give them their due and never confuse between the two. Thereby, we shall "render unto Caesar the things that are Caesar's, and unto God the things that are God's."[17] And it seems only proper that on a topic of such import as human intelligence, we should end on a messianic note. But in doing so, let me add one more messianic injunction of monumental significance: "Ye are the Salt of the earth, but if the salt have lost its savor, wherewith shall it be salted."[18] Seeking one's own "salt" is the work of living intelligence, perhaps the only true task. The artificial, the fake, the inauthentic cannot seek its saltiness (self-nature) for there is none—it is inauthentic by definition. The above two messianic injunctions correspond to the findings in this book of the core axes of ontological difference, namely, the *threptic* and the *perichoretic*. The former alludes to the source vitality of the organic consciousness (the saltiness) which provides the matrix of organic emergence; the latter alludes to the fact that organic emergence is always a mix of two things or levels, namely, the sacred and the profane (God and Caesar).

[17] Mark 12:17, *The Bible* (KJV).
[18] Ibid., Matt. 5:13.

Index[1]

[1] Note: Page numbers followed by 'n' refer to notes.

K. Roy, *Education, "Artificial" Intelligence, and Cognition*,
https://doi.org/10.1007/978-3-031-82263-6

The manufacturer's authorised representative in the EU is Springer Nature Customer Service Centre GmbH, Europaplatz 3, 69115 Heidelberg, Germany. If you have any concerns regarding our products, please contact ProductSafety@springernature.com

Printed and bound by CPI Group (UK) Ltd, Croydon, CR0 4YY
01/10/2026
02225912-0001